One Hundred Years of Solitude

MODES OF READING

TWAYNE'S MASTERWORKS STUDIES

Robert Lecker, General Editor

One Hundred Years of Solitude

MODES OF READING

Regina Janes

TWAYNE PUBLISHERS
A DIVISION OF G. K. HALL & CO.

One Hundred Years of Solitude: Modes of Reading
Regina Janes
Twayne's Masterworks Studies, No. 70

Published by Twayne Publishers
A division of G. K. Hall & Co.
70 Lincoln Street
Boston, Massachusetts 02111

Copyediting supervised by Barbara Sutton.
Book production by Gabrielle B. McDonald.
Composed in 10 on 14 Sabon with Eurostile Extended display
by World Composition Services of Sterling, Virginia.

First published 1991.
10 9 8 7 6 5 4 3 2 1 (hc)
10 9 8 7 6 5 4 3 2   (pb)

The paper used in this publication meets the minimum requirements of
American National Standard for Information Sciences—Permanence of Paper for Printed Library Materials, ANSI Z39.48-1984. ∞™

Printed and bound in the United States of America.

Library of Congress Cataloging-in-Publication Data

Janes, Regina, 1946–
    One hundred years of solitude : modes of reading / Regina Janes.
        p.   cm.—(Twayne's masterworks studies ; no. 70)
    Includes bibliographical references and index.
    ISBN 0-8057-7989-2 (hc : alk. paper).—ISBN 0-8057-8038-6 (pbk.
: alk. paper)
    1. García Márquez, Gabriel, 1928–   Cien años de soledad.
I. Title. II. Series: Twayne's masterwork studies ; no. 70.
PQ8180.17.A73C5325   1991
863—dc20   90-28481
                                                                CIP

CONTENTS

CONTENTS

NOTE ON THE REFERENCES AND ACKNOWLEDGMENTS

The editions of *One Hundred Years of Solitude* cited in the text are Gregory Rabassa's translation (New York: Harper & Row, 1970) and Jacques Joset's third, annotated (Spanish) edition (Madrid: Cátedra, 1987).

I would like to thank Lowell Boyers for permission to reprint his drawing, Sophie Baker and Harper & Row for permission to reprint her photograph, and, especially, Steve Goodwin for returning Melquíades to his mother tongue. I should also like to remember some of the students who have helped me read and write and think about García Márquez: Mary Bellino, Lisa Crosby, Jennifer Kent, Denise Lynch, Patricia Fonseca, Licia Esposito, and Denise Ostrow. The book itself is for Dale and Zeb, who waited for it to be over.

Gabriel García Márquez.
Photograph by Sophie Baker.
Courtesy of Sophie Baker and Harper & Row.

CHRONOLOGY:
GABRIEL GARCÍA MÁRQUEZ'S LIFE
AND WORKS

1928   In Aracataca, Colombia, Gabriel José García Márquez is born
6 March to Luisa Santiaga Márquez Iguarán and Gabriel Eligio
García. The first of twelve children, Gabriel is left with his
maternal grandparents, Tranquilina Iguarán Cotes and Col.
Nicolás Ricardo Márquez Mejía, a Liberal veteran of the War
of a Thousand Days. On 6 December, in the Ciénaga train
station, striking banana workers are fired on by troops from
Antioquia. Casualty estimates range from 9 to 3,000 dead.

1929   Proceedings in the banana zone are denounced by the Liberal
legislator Jorge Eliécer Gaitán, defending the workers. By the
time García Márquez reaches high school, the episode has
disappeared from his history textbooks.

1936   García Márquez's grandfather dies; his blind grandmother is
increasingly helpless. Returns to his parents' home in Sucre
(until 1952), site of many non-Macondo stories, home of Mercedes Barcha.

1938–1940   Attends the Jesuit Colegio San José in Barranquilla.

1940   Obtains a scholarship to study at the Colegio Nacional at
Zipaquirá, near Bogotá.

1946   Finishes secondary education at Zipaquirá. Admires poets of
the *piedra y cielo* ("stone and sky"): Eduardo Carranza, Jorge
Rojas, and Aurelio Arturo, a group influenced by Juan Ramón
Jiménez and Pablo Neruda.

Enters the law school at the National University in Bogotá.

Among his fellow students are Plinio Apuleyo Mendoza and Camilo Torres Restrepo. Reads Kafka.

1947　First story, "The Third Resignation," published in *El Espectador*, a leading Liberal newspaper.

1948　Assassination of Jorge Eliécer Gaitán, Liberal presidential candidate, on 9 April, precipitates the *bogotazo*. Three days of riots destroy García Márquez's *pension* and manuscripts, close the National University, and set off *la violencia*, an undeclared civil war between Liberals and Conservatives that takes at least 250,000 lives between 1948 and 1964. García Márquez studies law at the university in Cartagena and takes up journalism. Publishes first journalistic article for *El Universal*, a new Liberal newspaper. Publishes more stories in *El Espectador* and reads Sophocles, Kierkegaard, and Claudel.

1950　Abandons legal studies and moves to Barranquilla. Writes the column "La Jirafa" for *El Heraldo*, a Liberal newspaper, under the pseudonym "Septimus." Joins the informal group of young writers around Ramón Vinyes, a Catalan refugee from the Spanish civil war, with Alvaro Cepeda Samudio, Germán Vargas, and Alfonso Fuenmayor. Group admires modernists such as Joyce, Woolf, and Hemingway, and introduces García Márquez to Faulkner. Vinyes returns to Barcelona and dies two years later, aged 66.

1952　First novel, *Leaf Storm*, rejected by Editorial Losada, Buenos Aires.

1954　Returns to Bogotá as a reporter (not a columnist) for *El Espectador*.

1955　"Un día después del sábado" wins prize of the Association of Writers and Artists of Bogotá. *Leaf Storm* published in Bogotá. Attends meetings of a cell of the Colombian Communist party. Travels to Geneva and Rome as a correspondent for *El Espectador*. Studies cinematography in Rome. Writes *In Evil Hour*, based on events in Sucre.

1956　Writes *No One Writes to the Colonel*. In Paris, learns that the dictator Rojas Pinilla has closed *El Espectador* and, later, its successor *El Independiente*. Cashes in return ticket sent by his former employers, secures some journalistic work, but has to collect bottles to defray the rent. Still falls behind on his bills. Has patient landlady.

1957　Travels in Eastern Europe with Plinio Apuleyo Mendoza. Becomes editor for *Momento* in Caracas.

Chronology

1958   Witnesses, 1–21 January, the fall of Pérez Jiménez, Venezuela's dictator since 1948 (seed of *The Autumn of the Patriarch*). Travels to Barranquilla 27 March, to marry Mercedes Barcha, who had been 13, he claims, when he first proposed. Writes for *Elite* and *Venezuela gráfica*. Publishes *No One Writes to the Colonel* in *Mito*.

1959   Fidel Castro's triumphant *guerrilleros* enter Havana 1 January. García Márquez becomes correspondent in Bogotá for Prensa Latina, the newly formed Cuban news agency. Attends the trial of Sosa Branco in Havana; joins other journalists in a petition for a review of the trial. Son Rodrigo born 24 August, baptized by Camilo Torres.

1960   Moves to New York City to manage the Prensa Latina office.

1961   Resigns as New York director of Prensa Latina. Travels to Mexico by bus through Mississippi (Faulkner country) to New Orleans. *In Evil Hour* wins Esso Literary Prize in Colombia. After August, writes no new fiction until January 1965.

1962   Publishes *Big Mama's Funeral* (short stories). *In Evil Hour* published in Madrid, with unauthorized changes of language. Author repudiates edition. Son Gonzalo born 16 April.

1963   Works for the Walter Thompson advertising agency in Mexico City. Writes screenplays, including *El gallo de oro* (The golden cock), based on a story by Juan Rulfo, with Carlos Fuentes. *Tiempo de morir* (Time to die) is filmed by Arturo R. Ripstein; Alberto Isaac adapts "En este pueblo no hay ladrones" (There are no thieves in this town).

1965   Writer's block breaks in January. Begins *One Hundred Years of Solitude*.

1966   Camilo Torres Restrepo dies in his first encounter with Colombian troops. Fragments of *One Hundred Years of Solitude* appear in Bogotá (*Eco*), Lima (*Amaru*), and Paris (*Mundo Nuevo*). Fuentes praises first three chapters in Mexico City (*Siempre!*). Editorial Sudamericana, Buenos Aires, proposes reissuing earlier works. First authorized edition of *In Evil Hour* published in Mexico.

1967   *One Hundred Years of Solitude* published by Sudamericana in June. 5,000 copies sold in 15 days; 500,000 in three and a half years. Moves to Barcelona in October to imitate, he claims, Vinyes's return to Catalonia.

1969   *One Hundred Years of Solitude* receives the Italian Premio Chianchiano and is named best foreign book in France.

1970   *One Hundred Years of Solitude* is published in English. Named
            one of the twelve best books of the year by *Time*. García
            Márquez declines Colombian government's offer of a consular
            post in Barcelona.

1971   Awarded honorary doctor of letters, Columbia University,
            New York City. Does not join other Latin American writers in
            protesting the Cuban government's treatment of the writer
            Heberto Padilla.

1972   Receives Rómulo Gallegos Prize, Venezuela. Gives prize money
            to MAS (*Movimiento al Socialismo*—Movement toward So-
            cialism), a Venezuelan party. Receives Neustadt Prize, awarded
            by *Books Abroad/World Literature Today* in Norman, Okla-
            homa. Publishes *Innocent Eréndira*.

1973   Assassination of president of Chile, Salvador Allende, in a
            brutal military coup 11 September. García Márquez decides to
            take a more active political role.

1974   Founds *Alternativa* in Bogotá, a left-wing magazine (runs
            through 1980). With Julio Cortázar, participates in the Russell
            Tribunal to publicize human rights abuses in Latin America.

1975   Publishes *The Autumn of the Patriarch*. Returns to Mexico
            City.

1976   Travels periodically to Havana. Prepares a book on daily life
            in Cuba under the U.S. blockade. Personal friendship with Fidel
            Castro.

1978   Attends signing of U.S.-Panama treaty in Washington, D.C. as
            a member of the Panamanian delegation. Personal friendship
            with Panamanian dictator Omar Torrijos. Founds Habeas, a
            human rights organization, in Mexico City.

1979   Member of UNESCO commission for the study of communica-
            tions problems in the Third World.

1981   Attends inauguration of Socialist President François Mitterand
            in France. Awarded the Legion of Honor. Seeks asylum at the
            Mexican Embassy in Bogotá after a warning that the Colom-
            bian military had accused him of conspiring with the M-19
            guerrillas. With *Chronicle of a Death Foretold*, breaks his
            vow to publish no more novels until Chile's military dictator,
            General Pinochet, falls.

1982   Awarded Nobel Prize for Literature. Assists in release of the
            poet Armando Valladares, political prisoner in Cuba since
            1960.

Chronology

1983   Starts a Colombian daily newspaper, *El otro,* with Nobel Prize money. Belisario Betancur's government guarantees García Márquez's safety in Colombia.

1984   Joins other foreign writers in protesting the U.S. McCarran-Walter Immigration and Nationality Act (1952), which permitted the State Department to deny admission to the United States to Communists, "subversives," or anyone whose "activities would be prejudicial to the public interest." (García Márquez had been excluded under the act, which was modified in 1987, since 1971.) Lives in Cartagena while writing *Love in the Time of Cholera.* Returns to Mexico.

1985   Publishes *Love in the Time of Cholera.*

1986–1988   Organizes and directs the Foundation of New Latin American Cinema in Havana and writes screenplays (including *Amores difíciles*) and a play *Diatribe of Love against a Seated Man.*

1989   Publishes *The General in His Labyrinth.* With Mexican poet Homero Aridjis, drafts a call signed by 28 Latin American intellectuals, including Fernando Botero, Carlos Fuentes, Rufino Tamayo, and Mario Vargas Llosa, for an international tribunal to judge "ecocide and ethnocide" in Brazil's Amazon basin. "To invoke national security to justify crimes against nature seems to us to be puerile and dishonest."

Literary and Historical Context

1

From Bloomsbury to Barranquilla; or,

Decolonizations and Liberations

I would be a very different author if, when I was twenty years old, I hadn't read this sentence from *Mrs. Dalloway:* "But there was no doubt that within (the coach) something great was seated; greatness that was passing, hidden, within reach of the common hands that for the first and last time found themselves so close to the majesty of England, the enduring symbol of the state that inquisitive archaeologists would identify in their excavations of the ruins of time, when London was no more than a street covered with grass, and when the people who were strolling its streets that Wednesday morning were scarcely a heap of bones with a few wedding rings, turned over in their own dust and the fillings of innumerable decayed teeth."[1]

Virginia Woolf's Bloomsbury is a long way from Aracataca, Colombia, or the bleakness of the Goajira peninsula where García Márquez remembers reading that sentence in a sweltering hotel room swarming with mosquitoes. But for the young writer who took *Mrs. Dalloway*'s damaged "Septimus" as pseudonym for his newspaper column in 1950, that sentence made a revolution: it showed how a single sentence could contain a cycle of civilization from fullness to decay. Forty years later, the mature laureate traced in the same sentence a hint for the destruction of Macondo and the hidden patriarch, works neither he nor his readers could have predicted of that young man reading, sweating, and swatting mosquitoes.

Aracataca is a small town in the foothills of a spur of the Andes, near the Atlantic coast. The town has a small railroad station, a river with clear water and large white boulders, a street of Turks, and a few African Colombians. It is not, however, surrounded by swamps: that is the town of Ciénaga ("swamp"), about 75 kilometers nearer the sea. There the massacre of striking banana workers memorialized in *One Hundred Years of Solitude* took place in 1928, when García Márquez was nine months old.

In the first few decades of the twentieth century, Aracataca knew a sudden, feverish, temporary prosperity generated by foreign capital when the notorious United Fruit Company invested in banana cultivation. By the time García Márquez was old enough to notice, the leaf-storm had subsided, and with it the town's prosperity. In summer Aracataca is dry and dusty, the sun unforgiving; in winter the rains come. This was the place whose memories, folklore, myths, characters, and history became Macondo's after Barranquilla (modern Colombian literary culture) met Bloomsbury (Western literary culture, Kafka and Proust, Tarzan and Tagore, Poe and Rimbaud).[2]

Cosmopolitan in his literary formation, hostile to the regional adventures of U.S. imperialism,[3] García Márquez developed as a writer in almost accidental exile, stranded in Paris when a dictator closed the newspaper that employed him. Abroad, he took up the major political issues for a Colombian of his generation—*la violencia* and its concomitants, the poverty, corruption, and exploitation that drove that period of undeclared civil war. Between 1948 and 1964 "the violence" killed at least 250,000 Colombians. *In Evil Hour, No One Writes to the Colonel,* and some of the stories of *Big Mama's Funeral* map the hopeless resistance to authority and the stoic endurance of the powerless against the period's stifling, oppressive backdrop. Then in 1959 came a political event that transformed Latin America's role in the world, enlarged Latin Americans' sense of opportunity, and provoked one of the worst periods of repression in Latin American history.

From Bloomsbury to Barranquilla

In January Fidel Castro and Che Guevara's *guerrilleros* entered Havana as Fulgencio Batista, the dictator long supported by the United States, fled. Two years later revolutionary Cuba defeated a U.S.-sponsored invasion at the Bay of Pigs. The neighboring colossus, looming for a century over the long green island, had developed a long crack. By 1962, when the United States threatened nuclear war over Soviet missiles in Cuba, an obscure island had become a central actor in world politics. Like Africa and Asia in the same postwar period, the Americas seemed at last to be "decolonizing." For almost 30 years Cuba figured as a source of inspiration for active revolutionary movements in Latin America and the Third World and for imitations of revolutionary movements in Europe and the United States.

Comparable in international impact to the French, Russian, and Chinese revolutions, the Cuban revolution seemed to augur the end of a dominance as oppressive as that which collapsed with the Berlin Wall, when Central Europe embarked on its postwar decolonization in 1989. Far from the front lines, Che Guevara's image adorned every student's room, and Fidel's cigar was more familiar than Groucho Marx's. The more enterprising called themselves "urban guerrillas" and kidnapped Patty Hearst. The more deadly called themselves "Red Brigades" and blew up German and Italian banks and bank presidents. During the 1960s guerrilla movements appeared from Guatemala to Argentina, by way of Nicaragua, Colombia, Bolivia, and Uruguay. Left-wing governments were elected in Brazil, the Dominican Republic, and, toward the end of the decade, Chile, when Salvador Allende became the first popularly elected Marxist president in the hemisphere.

The prospect of social revolution was not universally pleasing, however, either to local elites, threatened by social change or to the United States, anxiously "containing communism" from Korea and Vietnam to the Americas. In 1964 the United States sent warships to wait off the coast of Brazil while the military overthrew the elected president, João Goulart; in 1965 it invaded the Dominican Republic after the "communist" Juan Bosch was elected; in 1973 it supported the coup that overthrew Chile's Allende.[4] By the mid-1970s most of

5

the region had fallen under military dictatorships, trained in counter-insurgency techniques by the United States. The repression was savage: men, women, and children "disappeared." Thousands were tortured in prisons or murdered by right-wing death squads. In the countryside, the army leveled villages for collaborating with *guerrilleros,* and *guerrilleros* murdered village leaders for collaborating with the army. *La violencia* had spread.

The situation changed again at the end of the 1980s as democratic institutions returned in Brazil, Argentina, Chile, and Uruguay; guerrilla movements continued or began in Guatemala, El Salvador, and Peru; and former *guerrilleros* embraced the electoral procedures of liberal democracy in Nicaragua and Colombia. Begun in 1965, *One Hundred Years of Solitude* appeared on the cusp of the first of these transformations, with hope near its meridian and repression rising.

García Márquez had followed the politics of his earliest writings into active work for the revolution from 1959 to 1961. Then, almost at the same time, he withdrew from the writing of fiction and from political activism. Until he began *One Hundred Years of Solitude,* he published no new fiction after "The Sea of Lost Time" (mid-1961), a luminous vision of an underwater world, filled with the untried possibilities of a world seen upside down. Meanwhile, bursting around him was "the Boom."

The literary equivalent of decolonization, the Boom was a decade of sudden, unexpected, and noisy international acclaim showered on several generations of Latin American writers. It is usually dated from 1961, the year Samuel Beckett and Jorge Luis Borges shared France's Formentor Prize. Major new writers appeared in Mexico, Cuba, Guatemala, Colombia, Peru, Chile, Argentina, Uruguay, Paraguay, and Brazil, and great older writers finally achieved international recognition for works written decades earlier. Poems, novels, and essays crossed national and linguistic boundaries within Latin America and then kept traveling, via translations, to other continents. When *One Hundred Years of Solitude* appeared in 1967, it became for many the capstone of the Boom, because of its merits, its phenomenal success, and its

magisterial and idiosyncratic summation of a hundred years of developments in Latin American writing. The Boom subsided, but it had
created more cosmopolitan audiences not only in Europe and North
America, but also, more importantly, in Latin America. Latin American
readers had at last begun to read Latin American writers with the
avidity they had once reserved for the French, the North Americans,
and Kafka.

"*One Hundred Years of Solitude.* A book I detest!"[5] The only
person who has ever said that with real passion is García Márquez. It
is more difficult to live down a success than to live down a failure.
Many readers expected one *One Hundred Years of Solitude* after
another, as if that novel had been patterned on a conventional rather
than an unrepeatable model. But true to his craft, García Márquez has
done something new in each work since 1967.

Responding, as did others, to the counter-revolutionary repression that turned Latin America into a vast military barracks in the
1970s, García Márquez turned to that peculiarly Latin American genre,
the novel of the dictator. In *The Autumn of the Patriarch* (1975) he
wove a dense and elaborate tapestry of the solitude of power—fantastic, horrible, comic, pathetic. The author's baroque inventions compete
with the grotesque inventions of reality: children's brigades diligently
sweep the country from one end to the other; the dictator pays off the
foreign debt by selling the sea to the Americans, who cut it up in
numbered pieces and carry it to Arizona. That dense structure of
incomparable, emblematic images took García Márquez eight years to
work, and he seems to resent the continued popular preference for
Solitude over his *Patriarch.*

Chronicle of a Death Foretold (1981) re-creates the perfect patterning of classical tragedy for a simple, primitive, ironic murder. The
end is known from the beginning as no one acts to prevent a murder
that no one wants to commit. *Love in the Time of Cholera* (1985)
returns to the episodic structure and romantic entanglements of *One
Hundred Years of Solitude.* Instead of closing itself off as that novel
does, it leaves a loop open at the beginning, and at the end the action

continues, forever. A history of the promiscuous fidelity of Florentino Ariza, an inconspicuous Don Juan, the novel also celebrates sexuality among sexagenarians, the Magdalena River, and Cartagena. Most recently, García Márquez has returned to the solitude of power in a luminous account of the last voyage of Simón Bolívar, the Liberator, down the Magdalena to his death on Colombia's Atlantic coast, *El General en su laberinto* (1989; The General in His Labyrinth). At 61, García Márquez has written his first historical novel, complete with concluding note and chronology. Unlike *Solitude* and the *Patriarch*, these later fictions do not use the fantastic to create emblems, irreducible images that resonate with historical, political, theological, psychological, or literary implications. Nor are their structures as intricate.

One Hundred Years of Solitude remains García Márquez's greatest novel, his summa. *The Autumn of the Patriarch* is more ambitious, but as Samuel Johnson complained of a work he admired greatly (*Paradise Lost*), none of us has ever lived in the hero's situation, and no one has ever wished the book longer. Although it is no more inventive or imaginative than the *Patriarch*, *One Hundred Years of Solitude* has greater range and variety of life. If *Solitude* succeeds because it takes readers into the Latin American bedroom for the first time (a dubious but useful proposition that García Márquez once endorsed as better than most critical propositions), then *Solitude* takes us into many more bedrooms than does the *Patriarch*. The artistic achievement of the later fictions should remind us, however, that *One Hundred Years of Solitude* was no accident of self-expression but the work of a serious craftsman, a writer attentive to form, to the sentence, o language, "the instrument you use to say things."

2

The Importance of the Work

Macondo exists. That is its magic.

—Salman Rushdie[1]

One Hundred Years of Solitude is not yet as old as García Márquez when he wrote it. So it is perhaps a little premature to speak of its continuing importance to generations of writers and readers. But of its importance to the readers and writers of its time, there can be no doubt. When the novel appeared in 1967, García Márquez's fellow Latin American writers and critics recognized it at once as a brilliant solution to many of the same problems they had been grappling with. The last word in formal sophistication, it retells the great American myth of discovery, founding, development, and decay. With sympathy, humor, irony, and beauty, the novel catches the painful contradictions and comic paradoxes of Latin America's reality. Because of its phenomenal popular success as well as its merits, it became the definitive novel of the Boom.[2]

For other Third World writers, *One Hundred Years of Solitude* suggested new ways to represent societies very different from García Márquez's Colombian coast. *Solitude* represented the marginal and the primitive, yet it neither adopted the superior perspective of the Western anthropologist nor imitated an imagined, alien innocence (as in William Golding's *The Inheritors*). Instead, García Márquez's narrator shuttled almost imperceptibly from one perspective to another, now imitating the naïveté of his characters, now commenting ironically on that naïveté. In this single, supple, pluralistic voice, many writers recognized their own ambivalent and difficult relationships with a traditional culture. In much of the world, the unimaginably old coexists with the unbearably new, in what V. S. Naipaul has called "half-made" societies. For writers conscious of straddling two cultures, nostalgia for a simpler, primitive past vies with wonder at the persistence of habits of thought, patterns of life, and modes of belief that surely ought to be extinct, mere harmless fossils. Instead, like the coelacanth or the crocodile, they are alive and powerful in the present. (For Salman Rushdie, with a price on his head for alleged blasphemies in *Satanic Verses,* the conflict of cultural values threatens life itself.) García Márquez turned puzzlement or outrage into ironic wonder, and he enhanced the strangeness of the real for writers as various as India (and England's) Rushdie and the United States' Toni Morrison.[3]

For readers everywhere, *One Hundred Years of Solitude* redefined what could be done in a novel. Most writers restrict themselves to what is visible or what could be visible. They do not "see and tell / Of things invisible to mortal sight" (*Paradise Lost* III: 54–55). "Freely ranging in the zodiac of his own [and, through reading, others'] wit," García Márquez, like Milton or Pope or Borges, expanded reality to include what women have only imagined, what men have only believed: God, angels, devils, sylphs, flying carpets, and infinite libraries. He improved on nature's world by bringing back the dead and reinvented forms that never were in nature, such as flying carpets and floating virgins. Such a free deployment of the imaginary asserted Macondo's reality to be unlike ours, while it made visible those aspects of our reality that are ordinarily obscured by the conventions of realism.

For all the strangeness of its physics, the novel of Macondo communicates great human insight, poetic power, and a profound tragicomic vision of the exuberant hopelessness of the human enterprise. Integrating psychological realism, symbolic events (both fantastic and realistic), and political purpose, the novel links the virtues of the great bourgeois novel of the nineteenth century with the overt "literariness" of the self-conscious, self-reflexive postmodern novel. The combination was—and remains—unique.

Like *Oedipus Tyrannos* or *The Alchemist, One Hundred Years of Solitude* is a book that could be written only once. Although every reader wants a sequel, "Macondo Revisited," the perfection of the book's design precludes a trip to the ruins twenty years later by an eighteenth Aureliano or an aging Gabriel.[4] If they should return, the fictive world they would find, though it might be peopled by Fellini ghosts, would be very different from that leveled so many years ago. What is inimitable in *One Hundred Years of Solitude* is its design: the perfect fit between the hyperbolic, ironic wonders of the narrative and the self-referential conclusion that justifies and motivates the texture of the narrative.

At the end of *One Hundred Years of Solitude,* what every reader secretly knows of all fictions is made explicit: the "world" into which he has entered in the fiction is a text. At the end of the novel, there is no *hors texte;* there is only reading. Since this is always true of the relationship between a text, its readers, and the world, an author cannot use it more than once. Nor would this self-reflexive gesture be appropriate in other contexts, where it would be tautological or insignificant. All men have parents; all books are written. Macbeth does not have to worry about who his parents are, but Oedipus does. As parentage makes itself a question in *Oedipus Tyrannos,* so the nature of fictive reality teases the reader throughout *One Hundred Years of Solitude.* Yellow flowers sift from the sky for the funeral of José Arcadio Buendía, while the sad cortege of Col. Gerineldo Márquez mires in a dreary rain: how can such incompatible events occupy the same space? That puzzle is solved when we learn that these events have happened in a book: that is where they are now, have always been, and will always be.

Reversing the direction of the "nonfiction novel," *One Hundred Years of Solitude* does not pretend to represent a documentary reality.

Instead, it represents a reality elaborated by the imagination, firmly bedded in social, historical, and psychological realities, but also deliberately, daringly, impudently invented. It makes the imaginative elaboration of reality, possible only through art, one of the aspects of reality that the fiction represents. Such gestures are characteristic of the critical, self-reflective literature of our time. They show that the text is a place where meanings are made, produced by writers and readers, and they restore artifice to art. Vindicating invention as fundamental to this fiction's exuberant vitality, design obtrudes to shatter the mirror in which we readers have lost ourselves. Yet that crazed and curious mirror, *One Hundred Years of Solitude*, reflecting both design and reality, always comes together again before our eyes. Reminding us of our own necessary complicity in all its tricks, its play, and its warnings, it shows us the door of the magic room, which is both a way in and a way out.

3

Critical Reception: At Last I've Found You

Not since *Madame Bovary* has a work been received with the simultaneous popular success and critical acclaim that greeted *One Hundred Years of Solitude* when it appeared in 1967. *Solitude* became the first Latin American "best-seller." Translated into 26 languages, it has reached millions of readers around the world, and the very popularity of the book makes some people uneasy.[1] García Márquez has muttered that he may be the Vargas Vila of his generation, and if the reader has not heard of that once enormously popular Colombian novelist (1860–1933), that is García Márquez's point. Since the triumph of modernism, readers and critics have grown accustomed to a distinction between popular trash and high, priestly, inaccessible art. A book that crosses over the line to blur the boundaries makes many uneasy, including the author. Something must be wrong somewhere. What is wrong, of course, is the assumption that pleasing must be a fault.

If the wider reading public consumed the novel as if it were Ursula's little candy animals, the author's peers had already hailed the novel with unparalleled generosity. By a few brief instants, the critical applause García Márquez had expected preceded the popular success that he had not anticipated. Early in 1966 García Márquez was a respectable writer, well known to serious students of contemporary Latin American fiction, but principally famous for a writer's block that had lasted four years.[2] Then García Márquez sent the first chapters of *One Hundred Years of Solitude* to the far more prominent Mexican novelist, Carlos Fuentes, who neither hesitated nor hedged. In the June 1966 *Siempre!* Fuentes announced, "I have just read eighty pages by a master."[3]

Other voices joined his. Pablo Neruda characterized García Márquez as a "river brimming with water," unequaled for marvelous, inexhaustible, easy narrative.[4] Alejo Carpentier praised García Márquez as one among many writers who had found "the formula to deprovincialize Hispanic American literature."[5] Julio Cortázar, revolutionary as an author as well as in his political sympathies, set up *One Hundred Years of Solitude* as the literary equivalent to the Cuban revolution. Like his own open, experimental, and fantastic fictions, *One Hundred Years of Solitude* revealed "masks and facets of reality" that could never be discovered in the quotidian.[6] Guillermo Cabrera Infante, García Márquez's witty antipodes in politics, aesthetics, style, and literary objectives, paid *One Hundred Years of Solitude* the great compliment of linking it with his wife Miriam Gómez. She had, he said, read it twice before she finished his own *Three Trapped Tigers* (1965). But the single most astonishing response to *One Hundred Years of Solitude* was that of Peru's finest modern novelist, Mario Vargas Llosa. Eight years younger than García Márquez and better known before the publication of *One Hundred Years of Solitude*, Vargas Llosa set to work on a massive biographical and critical study of the Colombian writer, complete with bibliographical apparatus: *Gabriel García Márquez: Historia de un deicidio* (1971).

Such a tribute from one major living writer to another is, as far as I know, unique in the annals of literature. Dryden wrote that Milton, his living contemporary, was better than Homer and Vergil combined, but he said it in six lines, not six hundred pages. What could motivate such an expenditure of time and intellectual energy?

Critical Reception

In 1966, while Anglo-Americans were lamenting the death of the novel and readers of the nouveau roman were hoping the end would come soon, Vargas Llosa was dancing on the grave with unseemly glee. Joyce and Proust were no more; now Europeans "only have Robbe-Grillet, Nathalie Sarraute, or Giorgio Bassani," while Latin America had writers such as Julio Cortázar, Alejo Carpentier, and Carlos Germán Belli. Contemporary Latin American writing was "more interesting, less lethargic, and more lively" than any in Europe.[7] When *One Hundred Years of Solitude* appeared the next year, Vargas Llosa saw a book that he had been waiting for without knowing that he was waiting.

What startled García Márquez's peers was the ambition and the achievement of his project. For Vargas Llosa, *One Hundred Years of Solitude* was a "total novel," a member of that "madly ambitious species that competes with reality on an equal basis, confronting it with an image qualitatively equivalent in vitality, vastness, and complexity."[8] If Vargas Llosa was taken by the totality of García Márquez's creation, Fuentes saw that García Márquez had discovered a new way to imagine Spanish America. No longer yoked to the dead past of a hated history, Spanish America had been "mythified." The weary old dichotomies, "civilization and barbarism," "history and myth," "reality and imagination," had been dissolved. Recovered for literature were both "real" and "fictive" history: "all the notary's proofs and all the rumors, legends, exaggerations, fables that nobody wrote down, that the old told to the children, that the gossips whispered to the priest, that the witches and the mountebanks reenacted in tents and plazas." All those elements of Spanish America's paradoxical reality had seemed lost to letters, "submitted forever to the heavy tyranny of Doña Bárbara" or (as Fuentes later translated his unkind allusion to Gallegos) to folklore, naturalist testimony, and ingenuous denunciation.[9] *One Hundred Years of Solitude* had reclaimed them for literature.

If Vargas Llosa focused on the elaboration of a counterreality and Fuentes on the reimagining of reality, Severo Sarduy, a Cuban novelist even more experimental (and structuralist, semiotic and poststructuralist) than they, applauded the novel for barring and abolishing "the outside world" and replacing external (physical) reality and internal (psychological) reality with "textual production" or writing. Sarduy pointed out the novel's foregrounding of writing, its pervasive intertextuality, and its double practice of synchrony and variations. Unlike the conventional realistic novel that obscures its "writtenness," its artifices, and its patterns, *One Hundred Years of Solitude* puts the practice of writing in the foreground. In the lives of characters, writing is one aspect of their reality, somewhat less conspicuous than their sex lives. In the life of the text, however, textuality is reality, and obtrusive, significant patterning breaks up the narrative surface to stop the sequential, linear movement of this fastest moving of fictions. Within *One Hundred Years of Solitude* the stasis of myth continually transforms itself into the dissemination of literature, the variations of the novel, and back again.[10] With their very different readings, each reflective of the writer-critic's own interests and obsessions, Fuentes, Sarduy, and Vargas Llosa demonstrated at the outset the deliberate and conspicuous multiplicity of *One Hundred Years of Solitude*.

Other critics praised García Márquez's rediscovery of "the lost art of story-telling" (Ricardo Gullón), his redefinition of the real (Gregory Rabassa), his penetration of the Latin American bedroom (Gustavo Álvarez Gardeazábal), and his recovery of lost and mythic worlds (Carmen Arnau, Salman Rushdie). As Gene Bell-Villada put it twenty years later, *One Hundred Years of Solitude* was one of those works that alter the "universe of novel-writing" and add to the "known inventory of accepted practices and possibilities."[11] But in spite of all these virtues, reaction to the novel was not universally positive.

Not everyone agreed with Vargas Llosa that the accessibility of the text to readers at all levels, to Severo Sarduy as well as to you and me, was a virtue. José Donoso, the brilliant, insidious Chilean novelist, has suggested more than once, and without ever naming so unseemly a vice, that the grudging reception by some of *One Hundred Years of Solitude* proceeded from envy. (It scarcely needs to be said that Donoso, a great psychological novelist, does not suffer from the vice he analyzes so delicately. He has no occasion.) In *The Boom: A Personal History* (1977), Donoso credited García Márquez with an unprecedented "triumph at the level of commotion and scandal." The scandal, he explained, was "a product, above all, of how unbearable it is to some people that a book of such literary quality can also be an unprecedented public success." In "Pages from a Novel: The Garden Next Door," Donoso invented such a person, a much rejected but not dejected narrator. "I was convinced I could salvage and transform [my manuscript, rejected by the formidable literary agent Nuria Monclus] into a masterwork far superior to the consumerist literature made fashionable by such figureheads and false-gods as García Márquez, Marcelo Chiriboga, and Carlos Fuentes."[12] Although García Márquez could not protect himself from the resentments of the less successful (apart from burning his book and dressing in sackcloth and ashes), other attacks he brought on himself.

Situating himself on the left revolutionary bank of Latin American political discourse, García Márquez criticized both Octavio Paz, the great Mexican poet and one of the great twentieth-century poets, and Miguel Angel Asturias, the Guatemalan novelist awarded the Nobel Prize in 1967, for collaborating with the establishments of Mexico and Guatemala. Thus prodded into irritation, Paz and Asturias poked back (in interviews, not in writing) with characteristic criticisms that pried into the vulnerable areas of García Márquez's achievement.

As brilliant a theorist as he is a poet, Paz responded with a thrust to the soft underbelly of García Márquez's fiction, the almost Jamesian absence of theory apart from the reality of the text itself. García Márquez, he said, is "a man without ideas—without ideas, *tout court*. ... What Pound used to call a 'diluter,' one who spreads and popularizes other people's discoveries."[13] Like Paz, Neruda found the text "easy," and many sophisticated readers are impatient with the novel's virtues: its accessibility, lucidity, and rapidity. García Márquez himself has charged his text with superficiality, and William Gass has located the problem in an essential enmity between narrative and thought.

Forced to discuss *One Hundred Years of Solitude* in a comparative essay on Spanish American novels of the Boom, Gass conceded that it was *the* novel of the Boom and solved every problem other writers had been struggling with. But he wanted to point out two other features of the novel: "Its ease and its emptiness."[14] To the complications of García Márquez's elaborate surface, not unlike the infinite reflections of mirrors facing each other, Gass preferred psychological and linguistic density: that illusory sense of ever deeper penetration into a mind, a consciousness, or a situation.[15] More to Gass's taste was the *Paradiso* of Cuba's José Lezama Lima.

If Paz and Gass can be taken to represent the line that finds *One Hundred Years of Solitude* shallow and superficial, Asturias may be allowed to lead those, more common in Latin America than Anglo-America or Europe, who find the text politically frivolous. Just as García Márquez once charged Borges with a "literature of evasion," so others have accused García Márquez of retreating into a world of fantasy and unreality and abandoning the political and social struggles of Latin America. Asturias complained that García Márquez was providing a formula "designed to prevent our novels from dealing with our own problems" and inviting "our future writers to conceal our tragedy." Blanco Aguinaga complained that *One Hundred Years of Solitude* exalted ignorance and myth and substituted symbol for reality.[16] Such a novel created passivity and stifled attempts to resolve the contradictions of Latin American politics and society. A number of critics urged García Márquez to return from fantasyland to the worlds of *Big Mama's Funeral, No One Writes to the Colonel,* and *In Evil Hour,* fictions in which he had engaged the political struggles of Colombia and the deprivations suffered by the powerless in a poor and violent country. This was the only line of criticism that García Márquez ever troubled to answer (see Chapter 11).

Those who have made political and aesthetic objections to *One Hundred Years of Solitude* do not charge that the novel is not well done. Instead, they suggest that the novel need not have been done at all. They want an altogether different kind of thing: *One Hundred Years of Solitude* unwritten and rewritten, either as *Paradiso* or as *No*

One Writes to the Colonel. But among those who would be distressed if time could be reversed and *One Hundred Years of Solitude* erased are the other writers in Latin America, Asia, Europe, and the United States who have found its example liberating in their own fictions.

As for those who write without writing novels, "since 1967 it's been raining without stopping in Macondo: translations, exegesis, commentaries, approximations, discussions."[17] Among the major contributions to the study of *One Hundred Years of Solitude* are the edition of Jacques Joset, the edition of the early journalism by Jacques Gilard, the structuralist analysis of Josefina Ludmer, the historical researches of Lucila Mena, the hermeneutic analysis of Donald Shaw, and perhaps the most beautiful single essay written about the novel, Emir Rodríguez Monegal's "*One Hundred Years of Solitude:* The Last Three Pages." Many, many critics have added to our information about the text or have suggested new ways to read it; every essay and every class bring some new illumination to a work described as a world "where all the labyrinth is flooded with light."[18] The conversation continues.

A Reading

आयो यः कुलवंशस्य स बद्धः पादपं प्रति ।
यो बालस्त्वन्तिमो जातः पुत्तिकाभिः स खाद्यते ॥

ādyo yaḥ kulavaṃśasya
sa baddhaḥ pādapaṃ prati   /
yo bālas tvantimo jātaḥ
puttikābhiḥ sa khādyate   //

El primero de la estirpe está amarrado en un árbol,
y al último se lo están comiendo las hormigas.

The first of the line is tied to a tree, and the last is being eaten by ants.

Sanskrit translation and calligraphy by Steve Goodwin. The translation uses the anuṣṭubh verse form typical of the epic—a 32-syllable form with four eight-syllable "feet" of flexible, though rule-governed, short—long patterns.

22

4

An Imaginary Garden with

Real Toads

And then he saw the child. He was a dry and bloated bag of skin that all the ants in the world were laboriously dragging toward their holes along the stone path in the garden (381; 490).

This image of an abandoned baby consumed by swarming ants sets in motion the last three pages of *One Hundred Years of Solitude*. A newborn, the last Aureliano, is abandoned by the midwife and his father beside his dead mother. When his father returns from a self-pitying debauch, he sees the baby, little Aureliano, dessicated and swarming with ants dragging him to their hole. It is a horrible scene, and most readers and critics fail to notice it. We all repeat the action of the careless father who becomes, through the death of his son, the last Aureliano, Aureliano Babilonia. Instead of acting to save what is left of his child, Aureliano retreats from the hideous and pathetic reality in front of him, now twice abandoned, to go read the miraculous manuscript whose contents have finally opened. Instead of thinking even for an instant that Aureliano ought to save what is left of his child, we hurry after him and slip into the room just as he barricades the door. All the reader regards about the scene or remembers about that baby is his transformation into text, into the epigraph that finally permits the reading of the manuscripts of Melquíades: "The first of the line is tied to a tree, and the last is being eaten by ants" (381; 490). Like Aureliano, we scarcely see the little body in our headlong pursuit of the pleasures of the text. It is a very tough ending for the novel, this last event that takes place in Macondo, outside the room of Melquíades. Why does García Márquez do it? Why does he almost end his book that way?

It is entirely deliberate. Literature is littered with bodies invented to be identified with and then slaughtered, from Hector to Mr. Biswas, from Gertrude to Little Nell or Madame Bovary. As critics, we conventionally justify our pleasure in the deaths of our heroes and heroines by the enlightenment their deaths (which are only fictions) have afforded us or the exquisite anguish their deaths have enabled us to suffer. Aureliano Babilonia does without the anguish, but no character in a fiction has ever been more "enlightened" by a death than he. Still, in the case of little Aureliano, the slaughter seems as gratuitous as it is grotesque.

The child must die to finish the line and the book, but there are many ways to nip a young doom in the bud. Any of the pretty inventions that grace death in *One Hundred Years of Solitude* might have opened the manuscript, a rain of flowers, a swarm of butterflies. Even a pig's tail would serve. Instead, the author chooses to mark the brutality, not the beauty, of this consummation.

The imaginary world with which García Márquez has delighted millions of readers answers to our own in irreducible horrors as well as delights. We all have our favorites among the playful inventions that liberate us from the usual constraints of realism: priests who levitate with cups of chocolate, beautiful idiotic virgins who float away with the family sheets, flying carpets and vanishing Armenians, a miraculous room untouched by time, and the massive, tattooed sex of José Arcadio. These examples, so often cited, are benign. But an equal list of improbabilities of a tougher sort could be made: insomnia plagues pursuing Indians expelled from their kingdom, the simultaneous assassination of 16 Aurelianos, an endless train carrying the corpses of 3,000 banana workers, a ghost who longs for the company of the man who killed him. Like the baby eaten by ants, such inventions impel us to ask what they mean and why they are there. Remote from the genial wish fulfillments, literary allusions, or "theological sarcasm" (Carmen Arnau's term) of the more benign inventions, these events trouble us. As a rule, we never demand explanations for our happiness, but we insist on having our miseries accounted for.

Such invented horrors resharpen aspects of reality blunted by familiarity or reveal facets of the quotidian blurred and smeared by inattention. The assassination of 16 Aurelianos makes strange the daily familiarity of government-run death squads that eliminate potential "subversives." The insomnia plague, consciousness without memory or power, masks a bit of common knowledge we often forget: that memory is fundamental to the texture of human social, cultural, and political existence. What do we learn if we "go to the ant[s]" in *One Hundred Years of Solitude?*

At the simplest level, the ants finish the theme of solitude. Nature reasserts her inhuman dominion. A single individual, Aureliano Babilonia, through his inaction, grief, and carelessness, brings an end to the line, and a family disappears forever. The cruelty of the means prevents a serene acceptance of the outcome: the image of the end is pain, darkness, and loss. The child is no longer even recognizably human as the ants, nature herself, exert their nonhuman power and desire. At the same time, this little death could easily have been avoided, so its horror counsels neither despair nor resignation, but exertion. Finally, the baby's death is put to a literary use that transforms it entirely (and literally—in the reading of the manuscripts, a dead child turns into a "mythological animal"). The death opens the book of Melquíades, but it qualifies the exhilaration of that very exhilarating and very literary ending. Our exuberance at the book's turning into a world, the world's turning into a book, is checked when we remember how we got there: it cost the life of a child, eaten by ants.

If we interrogate those ants, they turn out to be very busy indeed. Meanings swarm from them, running about as rapidly and in as many different directions as from any disturbed ant heap poked with a stick or an interpretive code. To reach the ants, the reader has called upon many different codes or categories of explanation to make sense of (to naturalize) the narrative's events—psychological, historical, literary, political, cultural. But each event, potentially, can also be run through most of those codes. In a novel that takes us through a cycle of human history (and intimates the futility of that history), the ants form a link to far greater cycles of no greater efficacy: "Other species of future animals would steal from the insects the paradise of misery that the insects were finally stealing from man" (378; 486). The ants call up a moment in evolutionary and geological time far beyond the temporal limits of the novel or a hundred human years; but that extinction to come is no less certain for its distance. In nature's great cycles, not even the insects are permanent.

Within the novel, the ants embody the natural forces that must be pushed back, struggled against, extirpated, if human order is to prevail. Nor are they a trivial antagonist: 30 percent of all living creatures in the tropics—and the most abundant and damaging predators—are ants or termites. "You can hardly place your hand on a tree trunk or hanging vine stem without disrupting the traffic of a trail of foraging ants."[2] Servants of decomposition, nature's essential deconstructors, they are the dominant species. When the struggle against them is given up, the end comes soon. The struggle against the ants parallels the struggle to maintain the incest taboo: both are attempts to maintain a specifically human social order. (In one of language's little fortuities, *incest* = *insect, incesto* = *insecto,* so the incest taboo is also an insect taboo. Among species, insects are particularly given to incest.) When the Buendías finally succumb to incest, they also succumb to the insects.

In Latin American fiction, nature's power relative to man is a common theme. Evoking the theme, the ants also evoke a literary tradition, the texts in which that theme has appeared. For García Márquez's Colombian predecessor, Eustasio Rivera, the jungle also was stronger than man, and it devoured him (*La Vorágine* [The vortex],

1924). As they bear away the baby, the ants carry along a theme common in Latin American fiction (civilization versus nature) *and* an allusion to a particular literary tradition. But those ants are still busy: they have barely begun to deliver their meanings.

Still closer in, the ants condemn the Buendías and their solitude. The last Buendía/Babilonia ends inside them, and the solitary race feeds a community of more successful social insects. Few signs of the failure of a community, of its fundamental breakdown, could be greater than this careless, unintentional abandonment of the young. In a birth, a community continues, and the continuing life of the community depends upon the care of the newly born, the basic social act. Even the exposure of a deformed infant has a motive in the community's sense of well-being. Aureliano's abandonment of his child has no motive save the indulgence of solitary self-pity. The solitary offspring disappears under the mandibles of a better organized, more cohesive community; the woman turns to stone.[3] For any community, no ending could be more final. All those generations of life, energy, and hope come to an end in this image, the dead baby. When the ants are done, there will be, as Melquíades predicted, no trace of a Buendía left in Macondo.

Through the image of a baby consumed by ants, both the futility of human effort and the necessity of human solidarity are simultaneously rendered. Only the ants (or a hurricane) could signify so purely the power of a nonhuman other. Only the ants (or a cyclone) could evoke the inhuman cycles of geological time or the ceaseless, hopeless human work of establishing a permanent human presence and order in unpropitious surroundings where the earth quakes, volcanoes erupt, hurricanes level, and rivers flood.

Yet if the ants show us how doomed and how hopeless all human efforts are, they also show us, better than a cyclone, how necessary those efforts are. No human effort can stop a cyclone, but human efforts usually, and without great difficulty, prevent babies from being eaten by ants. As a character, Aureliano Babilonia may have been unable to do anything besides abandon his child, however briefly. But a little paternal responsibility, a little midwifely attention, a little network of social obligations, and the ants would have had to dine elsewhere. Human beings cannot prevent the great cosmic and geological disasters, but there are other disasters, smaller in scale, human in origin, and great enough for mankind, that lie within the control of a human community and human solidarity.

But there is something still more peculiar about those ants dragging away that baby. No one notices it as the fate of a child, and no one pays attention to the child. Leading readers by the nose, the narrator induces them to pass by rapidly, hurriedly, in a rush for the manuscript. Aureliano Babilonia notices his child, but only as it enables him to decode the manuscript. Those busy little ants have thus also provided a complex, multilayered fable of reading. Reading is everything, that fable suggests, but it is not enough.

Even as the reader's and Aureliano's attention is funneled to the manuscript, away from the child, the presence of the child shows the inadequacy of reading by itself. When Aureliano sees the child being dragged away, he is frozen. Not with horror, but because he suddenly sees and understands the epigraph of the manuscript: "The first of the line is tied to a tree, and the last is being eaten by ants." The epigraph of the manuscript thus becomes the epitaph of the novel. What opens the one, closes the life of the other. Now, Aureliano has spent months and years trying to decipher the manuscripts. In solitude, he has consumed countless books and much of his life in the attempt to decode those parchments. Study, reading, and attention have enabled him to identify the grammar of his text, and they were essential prior conditions to its comprehension. After all his reading and study, however, it is neither reading nor study that provides the key that opens the manuscripts. When he finally reads them, it is a momentous experience in his own life that enables him to do so. He sees his child being eaten by ants. Without that confirmation in his experience, the epigraph to the manuscript would remain just a puzzling form of words that do not signify anything at all. Aureliano would still be unable to read it.

Our ants thus provide a bizarre, and not altogether pleasant, example of the way we all use our lived experiences in order to read.

An Imaginary Garden with Real Toads

We cannot help bringing more to books than just our reading, but we notice the reciprocity between reading and experience only when a change in our experience produces a radical change in our reading, as it has for Aureliano Babilonia. At the same time, the episode affirms that experience without reading is meaningless. Without Aureliano's reading, reading, and more reading, the horror of the child's death would remain only an experience of horror, brutal and unassimilated. Through the horror of that instant he is at least enabled to understand something beyond the moment and beyond himself.

Just as we begin to congratulate ourselves, however, the ants pull us back. For they also demonstrate the dangerous, seductive power texts have over us.

Our experience and our moral sense should have made us stop dead in the presence of the dead baby. But neither was awake. By making us read over the episode, by leading us past it without our noticing what we have disregarded, García Márquez has demonstrated, a little unkindly, the power of the text. In the dried skin of the baby, critics have noted the parchments' resemblance to human skin. To see only a manuscript in the skin of a dead baby is perhaps to make reading too important, a congenital or professional failing of literary critics. (Not to see the skin of the manuscript in the skin of the baby is to miss a delicate point. We cannot win this one.) This text, any text, can make us disregard horror, treat it as merely bizarre, subordinate it to our own ruling passions and dominant ideas, or enjoy it immensely as an aesthetic experience. Would any reader of *One Hundred Years of Solitude* trade the life of that baby eaten by ants for the reading of the manuscript? Would any reader consent never to know what is in the manuscript in order that the child live happily—or unhappily—ever after?

Reading may make us more passive as we swallow whole horrors unchewed; there is no reason literature should be less effective as an opiate than religion or television. Or reading may end in the self-delighted contemplation of our own interpretations. As soon as we know why, textually speaking, a baby is eaten by ants, we feel better about some babies, textual babies, being eaten by ants. Explanations always comfort us: we feel better about serial killers when we have blamed their mothers, and better about earthquakes when we have analyzed the movement of the plates. Or reading may lead to the probing of the aesthetic experience itself: if the text slips us past the dead baby, it is also the text that trips us as we skip past. It is easy to read past the last death in the last dawn of Macondo, but that hard little image mocks our obliviousness, whether or not we see it.

Now perhaps we can let those ants go about their business. They are part of the world that García Márquez has invented in *One Hundred Years of Solitude,* and what they tell us will depend on what we ask of them. The only additional thing we might ask is that they tell us one thing, and one thing only. That, of course, is the one thing they will not do. Pressed to limit their meanings, they may assert their *ant*ness and refuse to say anything at all. Silence or dissemination: those are the possibilities. But if, arbitrarily, we were to make one point about that hard, thoughtless little image on which we stub our moral toes, it would be that García Márquez simultaneously surprises us and makes us think. His text draws us into itself to account for its events, and it thrusts us out to consider in other contexts the meanings of its events. As the Argentine novelist Beatriz Guido put it, this book so impeccable as literature is also a very strong book that says the most terrible things.[4]

Those busy little ants work impeccably as literature: they make a sharp and luminous image that astonishes and surprises. They ground the concept of natural cycles, and in their final appearance they show the transforming power of the smallest, slightest, most specific detail. At the same time, they tell us terrible things about the failure of individuals, the disappearance of families, and the endless cycles of repetitions and annihilations to which nature condemns us. At the end, having dispersed over so much terrain and explored so many places, they lead both Aureliano and us back into the book. There they remain, ready to formicate again at the thrust of an interpretation. Dragging their baby down the stone path, the ants also belong in García Márquez's imaginary garden.

5

A Myth of Origins for a Mythic Novel

There is a story García Márquez tells about how a certain famous novel came to be written. When he barricaded himself in the study of his house in Mexico to write *One Hundred Years of Solitude,* he did so because of a vision. On the road to Acapulco, driving his Opel with his wife and children, he suddenly had a revelation: he saw that he had to tell his story the way his grandmother used to tell hers, and that he was to start from that afternoon in which a father took his child to discover ice. The car made a U-turn on the highway, they never reached Acapulco, and 15 months later García Márquez emerged from his study with a manuscript in his hands to meet his wife Mercedes with the bills in hers. They traded papers, and she put the manuscript in the mail to Editorial Sudamericana.

In the barricaded room and the sudden revelation of a sentence, the attentive reader will see a parallel to the experience of the last surviving Aureliano. Any reader who also writes may recognize something else in the experience of the last Aureliano: the sickening sensation of absolute certainty that he will never be able to get out of this narrative, that he is trapped in it forever, that it will never, ever finish.

(The gleeful tone of the narrator writing *about* Aureliano as Macondo vanishes into the book must be that of the writer who knows this book is almost, at last, finally, over "from time immemorial and forever more.")

Like the stories García Márquez tells inside his novel, this story leaves out many details we would expect in a realistic account of how the novel appeared. Omitted are such matters as the interviews García Márquez granted while writing the book; the sending of early chapters of the completed manuscript out for review; the early praises of the book the year before it was published; the negotiations under way in 1966 to reprint his earlier writings on the basis of expectations about the work in progress. The story as García Márquez tells it ends on a tense note of uncertainty as the completed manuscript is entrusted to the post.

Not only does García Márquez leave out the "real life" politics of his book's appearance, but he also skips past the actual work of writing. If the story of *One Hundred Years of Solitude* begins with a myth, it ends with a mystery. When he received word that the book had arrived at the publisher, the author removed all trace of its passage through the world: "Mercedes helped me throw away a drawerful of working notes, diagrams, sketches, and memoranda. I threw it out, not only so that the way the book was constructed shouldn't be known—that's something absolutely private—but in case that material should ever be sold. To sell it would be selling my soul, and I'm not going to let anyone do it, not even my children."[1] This anecdote may tell us more about García Márquez as a person and a writer than the more famous myth of the road to Acapulco.

His reference to diagrams and sketches points to the careful planning of *One Hundred Years of Solitude;* the working notes and memoranda may be vanished traces of the basis in reality that García Márquez claims for every event in the novel. In the possibility (or certainty, in today's world of competing archives) that the working materials might be sold, commercial acumen appears, as does the author's confidence in the success of his book. The determination to prevent such a

A Myth of Origins for a Mythic Novel

sale marks a not uncommon aversion to the commercialization of artistic activity; but actually destroying the materials, then recounting the destruction, is less common. Making the sale of his working materials impossible, García Márquez cut himself off from the constitutive elements of his past, much as male characters do throughout *One Hundred Years of Solitude*. (José Arcadio Buendía axes the alchemical laboratory; Colonel Aureliano Buendía burns his poetry; Aureliano Segundo smashes the porcelain—each destroys an aspect of his self-definition.) Most striking, however, is the suggestion that the completed novel is a mask. García Márquez has denied access to the discarded fragments, not because he values art and the finished product over any process of construction, but because there is a soul in the fragments. From the ultimate privacy of writing itself he has shut out editors, biographers, and critics.

If the story of the turning Opel on the road to Acapulco leaves out a great deal, it does tell the story García Márquez meant to tell. It relates a myth (in the loose sense of an archetypal story) of solitary dedication in the service of an insight, a labor of solitude and isolation. And it focuses all our attention on the moment when, from nowhere, from out of the air, there suddenly descended a solution to the problem the author had long been struggling with. The problem was how to turn the remembered world of Aracataca into a book, how to write that world. The solutions were the discovery of a tone, the proper language for the fiction, and the initial event, the point from which to begin to tell the story.

García Márquez had wanted to write the story that became *One Hundred Years of Solitude* since adolescence, when he revisited with his mother the house of his grandparents in Aracataca. As an infant, García Márquez had been left in Aracataca in the care of his maternal grandparents, Col. Nicolás Ricardo Márquez Mejía[2] and Tranquilina Iguarán Cotes. Cousins, from Riohacha, the colonel and his wife had settled in Aracataca at the end of the War of a Thousand Days (1899–1902), a few years before the "leafstorm." Along with many other adventurers, the leafstorm brought a new telegraphist to town, Gabriel

33

Eligio García. He soon fell in love with Luisa Santiaga Márquez Iguarán, the daughter of the colonel and his wife, but the match was
opposed by her parents.

Not only was the fellow a rootless newcomer, but he was also a
member of the Conservative party, the traditional antagonist of the
Liberal party. The colonel was a Liberal by party affiliation; he had
fought on the Liberal side in the War of a Thousand Days under Gen.
Rafael Uribe Uribe, and he had been present when the treaty was signed
at Neerlandia. The Liberals had lost that war to the Conservatives, as
they had lost almost every conflict since 1860. Not choosing to lose
their daughter to the leafstorm and a Conservative, the girl's parents
removed her from temptation by sending her on a long trip. But the
amorous telegraphist secured the cooperation of other sentimental
telegraphists on the route and contrived to communicate his continuing
passion from afar. (The episode figures in *Love in the Time of Cholera*.)
Eventually, the parents permitted the marriage, the young couple settled in Riohacha (where the telegraphist had been transferred), and the
rift was healed when Luisa returned to Aracataca in December 1928
to give birth to her first son, Gabriel José García (for the telegraphist)
Márquez (for his mother's father, the colonel).[3] When Luisa returned
to her husband, she left Gabriel—"Gabo," or "Gabito"—in Aracataca
with his grandparents. He would remain there until the death of his
grandfather when he was eight.

In "the abandonment by his parents . . . [to] the big rambling
house of his grandparents," Emir Rodríguez Monegal finds the roots
of García Márquez's fiction.[4] García Márquez's anecdotes of childhood
recall a big house full of ghosts and dead people, with conversations
in code and prodigious terrors. There was an empty room where
Aunt Petra had died, and another where Uncle Lázaro had died. He
remembers being seated in a corner at six o'clock one night and being
told not to move: "If you move, Aunt Petra will come out of her room,
or Uncle Lázaro, who is in the other." The child did not move. There
was another, very lively aunt, always busy, always consulted by townsfolk over mysteries. A boy brought her a hen's egg with a protuberance.

She looked it over solemnly, announced that it was a basilisk's egg, and ordered it burned in the courtyard. The same aunt set herself to weave a shroud, and when her nephew Gabriel asked why, she replied, "Because I am going to die, my son." When she finished the shroud, she went to bed and died. They buried her in the shroud.

There are also less spectral anecdotes. The colonel was a big, vigorous, gregarious man (closer to the physical type of the novel's Aureliano Segundo than Col. Aureliano Buendía). The house was full of guests, as well as ghosts. Among the guests were several natural sons of the colonel from his period of wandering during the war. The colonel took his grandson to the circus to see the dromedary and gave him a zoology lesson from the dictionary. When he realized that his grandson had never seen ice, he took him over to the banana company camp, ordered a case of frozen red snapper opened, and had his grandson put his hand on the ice. Having killed a man in a duel in Riohacha, he knew "how much a dead man weighs." His house was shaded by almond trees, and his patio was filled with flowers.

After he died, the boy was taken away from Aracataca to live with his parents. His grandmother had cataracts and was going blind. She was also becoming senile, and after Gabriel left, the house fell into decay. The almond trees were destroyed by ants, the flowers disappeared from the garden.

Word of his grandmother's decrepitude had reached the family from friends before her death. After she died, when he was about 15, Gabriel returned to Aracataca with his mother to sell the house in which they had both grown up. The return was a formula for nostalgia: a lively and beloved past confronted a dilapidated, disillusioning present. If, as Rodríguez Monegal maintains, García Márquez had first been abandoned by his parents, he duplicated his losses again and again. First there was the loss of his mother, then at eight of his grandfather. When he lost his grandfather, he lost the rest of his childhood as well: his room, his house, his friends, his Montessori school, his grandmother. For that familiar place, he got in trade a mother he had known briefly and at rare intervals, a houseful of unknown siblings, and an unfamiliar father. Later, when his grand-mother died during his adolescence, he lost to the ravages of time and reality even the idealized childhood memory of that house. More important than any individual loss was the pattern of losses, repeating themselves at intervals. From that return to a hot, desolate town under a merciless sun, García Márquez traces the initial desire to write the story of his house, his town, and his region.

The novel was to be called *La casa* (The house), and the earliest traces of it appear in the author's journalism of the 1950s as "Notes for a Novel," which, significantly, he always published under his own name, not under the pseudonym used in his column. Among the earliest pieces appears "The House of the Buendías," occupied by Col. Aureli-ano Buendía and his wife Doña Soledad, their son Tobías, and their daughter Remedios. An odd first-person fragment told from a child's point of view anticipates the interior monologues of *Leaf Storm*. Re-turning to church newly and dangerously decked out in too much finery, the runaway servant Meme is rescued from hostile townsfolk by "my father's" firmness.[5] Most of the early fictions contain elements that reappear in the later novel; in fact, it is difficult to find an early story that has not left a trace in *One Hundred Years of Solitude*. (Jacques Joset's edition points out many of them.) A similar claim might be made for much of the early journalism (well treated by Raymond L. Williams in his *Gabriel García Márquez* [1984], as well as by Joset).

Inventing and reinventing Macondo was the work of more than 15 years. "Macondo" is the name of a banana plantation near Araca-taca; it means "banana" in Bantu, and as Gaston discovers, to his dismay, it is homonymic with Africa's Makonde. By 1952 Macondo had become the town in *Leaf Storm*, García Márquez's first novel. It is also the setting for "The Monologue of Isabel Watching It Rain in Macondo," "One Day after Saturday," and "Big Mama's Funeral." Unnamed, but identified by the presence of the widow Rebeca, it is the setting for "Tuesday Siesta." It is also the town the Colonel (to whom no one writes) left in 1906, 50 years before his story begins, when the banana fever arrived. He took the same little yellow train that reappears in *One Hundred Years of Solitude.* "One Day after Saturday" (written 1955, published 1962) inaugurated the deadpan, twisted realism of the later novel, and it is retold in its entirety, from the rain of dead birds to the Wandering Jew, at the end of *One Hundred Years of Solitude.* Macondo was preeminently the town desolated by the leafstorm that the train had brought, the town of the grandfather and the child, the town of the banana fever. The other stories are all set elsewhere.

The final Macondo sweeps up themes, subjects, attitudes, images, and motifs that had first appeared in very different artistic contexts and styles. Realistic representations of political resistance reappear from *No One Writes to the Colonel, In Evil Hour,* and "One of These Days," and allegorical invention from the phantasmagoric account of Mr. Herbert's foreign exploitation in "The Sea of Lost Time" (the last story García Márquez completed before *One Hundred Years of Solitude).*[6] In *One Hundred Years of Solitude* Álvaro retells "Night of the Curlews," an extended metaphor for the denial of political violence: curlews peck out the eyes of three men, and all the world denies that it ever happened. Motifs less political and more personal include Meme deserted by her lover, with only her blind grandmother sensing her trouble ("Artificial Roses"). An old woman's senility grieves the three who care for her ("Bitterness for Three Sleepwalkers"). A woman returns to the house where many years ago she played with a boy who waits for her in death; she restores the house, and he narrates the tale ("Someone Has Been Disarranging These Roses"). Burial alive, doubles, even twins who have the same lover in a story by Mark Twain, all make appearances in the early fictions or the journalism. Though none originally takes place in Macondo, they all make their way there for *One Hundred Years of Solitude.*

When García Márquez came to write *One Hundred Years of Solitude,* he took with his own earlier texts the same freedom all writers take with life and others' writing. He stole, he borrowed, and he recombined. He reimagined the possibilities of literature, and the literature he reimagined included his own. He had served a rigorous apprenticeship to his craft in which he mastered his medium, explored different styles, and gradually moved closer to the peculiar blend of the real and the imaginary that characterizes *One Hundred Years of Solitude*. But between the earlier fictions and the "total" reality—personal, cultural, political—of the later novel there lies a long silence. Elements of style, atoms of detail, had made their appearance, but they were waiting for a form and a language. Familiarity with those earlier texts enhances one's appreciation of the magnitude of García Márquez's achievement in the later novel because the difference between them is so vast. It becomes clear why that experience on the road to Acapulco was so momentous.

6

A Pig's Tail, a Pig's Eye

I merely wanted to tell the story of a family who for a hundred years did everything they could to prevent having a son with a pig's tail, and just because of their very efforts to avoid having one they ended by doing so.[1]

García Márquez tells stories for a living; he should almost never be believed. Anyone who has read *One Hundred Years of Solitude* knows that this innocent explanation does not hold water. It is not that the story is about important things and he is suggesting that it is about something unimportant. It isn't that. It is that the baby with a pig's tail is born to a couple who have never heard any warnings against incest and pigs' tails. Aureliano's grandmother, Amaranta Ursula's mother, Fernanda, keeps them ignorant of the precise details of their relationship, but she has no fear of incest and no interest in pigs' tails, and she makes no effort to inhibit the one or the other. The text does not sustain the causal suggestion García Márquez makes here. Let's try again.

"I wanted only to give a poetic permanence to the world of my childhood, which as you know took place in a large, very sad house, with a sister who ate dirt and a grandmother who predicted the future, and numerous relatives with the same name who never made much distinction between happiness and madness."[2]

This sounds much more like it. "The world of my childhood": a vanished world, like Macondo, destroyed inevitably by the simple

39

passage of time and not by anyone's fault. To its river with white boulders, its little train station, the house filled with ghosts, the now silent grandmother and the dead grandfather who took little Gabo to the circus to see a dromedary, to all these *One Hundred Years of Solitude* gives "a poetic permanence." This is it, this has to be it. But just a minute; there's something wrong with that dirt-eating sister and her prognosticating grandmother.

Those people are not in García Márquez's biography, in his life; they are in his text. From the sister who ate dirt to the end of the sentence, García Márquez is lifting material from his novel and, in the process, mocking biographical critics who ferret out of the life only what they have already found in the fiction. The real "world of my childhood" disappears forever; only the fiction remains, replacing the world it was meant to make permanent. Donning his mask, García Márquez once again erases the boundary between the real and the imaginary so that "no one knew where the limits of reality lay." He has, yet again, told a story.

It is notoriously difficult to get a grip on the "one thing" that *One Hundred Years of Solitude* is "about." García Márquez may be excused for his failure to provide a convincing or adequate account since he wrote the book and we cannot ask him to do all our work for us. Critics writing essays on a particular aspect of the text or on a particular question evade the issue easily: their orientation to the text is defined by the problem they have in hand. Nor is it a problem for readers who hold with Roland Barthes that a text is not an apricot but an onion: not a fruit with a hidden kernel, but "a construction of layers (or levels or systems) whose body contains, finally, no heart, no kernel, no secret, no irreducible principle, nothing except the infinity of its own envelopes—which envelop nothing other than the unity of its own surfaces."[2] But it is a problem for the critic who presumes to introduce the text. Critics in this position, at this moment, almost always collapse into plot summary. Or they pretend there is no problem and proceed to plot summary. But there is, if not a problem, a critical issue in the text's elusiveness.

A Pig's Tail, a Pig's Eye

One of the novel's principal achievements is a structure that prevents any of the usual leading candidates for organizing meaning from emerging as primary (see Chapter 9). Episodic and cyclical, *One Hundred Years of Solitude* has a subject in the chronicle of a town, Macondo, a founding family, the Buendías, and their house. As founders and builders, the Buendías antedate the town and the house, but following the initial act of foundation (after which the novel begins) they prosper, decline, and disappear together. With the disappearance of the town, the family, and the house, a great cycle is completed. A fragment of man's historical time disappears, and nature—those ants—reasserts itself. The shape of the whole gives a sense of the novel's scope, but not of causes or meanings. For those we look to plot, the pattern of action. In the always threatening incest that culminates in the birth of a child with a pig's tail, the novel has the semblance of a plot. But the wise reader will not invest all his intellectual capital in that plot line. It is a parody of a plot (a very famous plot) that displaces the significance we still expect from plotting. According to Borges, magic's causality, where every particular predicts, makes better novels than nature's endless, unpredictable flux. Echoing but deepening Borges's dictum, the magical plot line of incest superimposes a single, seemingly inevitable causality over the accidental, uncontrollable, and infinite operations of nature.[3]

The busy surface of the novel, foregrounding every code, prevents any single code from taking precedence over the others. As García Márquez described his project, he meant in *One Hundred Years of Solitude* to go beyond the social and political reality of his own country to "all the reality of this world and the other, without preferring or depreciating any of its aspects."[4] The effect is an unceasing competition for (interpretive) attention.

We can see this conflict in the title itself. "One hundred years" suggests history, a temporal span, and a cycle, as if we should look to time and history for the novel's meanings. When we look, we find a comical and satirical account of the tragic futility of Macondo's history. García Márquez has recounted the central myth of Latin American

41

history: great hope betrayed, and betrayed again, but still not entirely ended. Although Macondo is destroyed with the Buendías at the end of the novel, Melquíades had found a prediction of a Buendía-less Macondo when he first began writing, and he tells José Arcadio Buendía about it (59; 130). José Arcadio Buendía dislikes that prediction, so Melquíades, comically, tactfully, never returns to the subject that so upsets his friend. The detail implies that Macondo endures beyond the Buendías and that places outlast families and their histories. (Aureliano Babilonia fails to notice Melquíades's first prediction in his reading, and the reader has long forgotten it. Aureliano may be too engrossed in his own story to notice something that does not tell him about himself, or he may be unable to read beyond himself.) The hundred-year history that has finished, however, names neither the family nor the town; it is one hundred years of "solitude," a timeless, metaphysical, ahistorical concept.

Unitary as a word or concept, "solitude" is never defined in the novel but splinters into many solitudes. There are solitudes of study, work, power, and love, as well as the great solitude of death and the greater solitude of oblivion. Solitary or shared, solitude may signify a narcissistic turning away from others or an abandonment by others. Negative insofar as it implies an absence of solidarity and community with other people, solitude is also a source of serenity, an end to pain, and a necessary (though not sufficient) means to insight. Principally human, solitude belongs also to places and to things, especially the relics of a human past. The word first appears clinging to the Spanish galleon discovered by José Arcadio Buendía. An emblem of past hope, discovery, and liberation from the old world to the new, the galleon is abandoned and desolate when José Arcadio Buendía finds it and burned out when his son Aureliano comes across it.[5] The title asks us to take the meaning of solitude as a timeless condition of the characters (and their town) just as seriously as we take the "hundred years" that that solitude lasts. If "one hundred years" makes us ask about history and the problems of Latin America, "solitude" makes us ask about the human condition and the characters who suffer their solitudes.

A Pig's Tail, a Pig's Eye

But something very odd happens if we apply the title to the novel. Most critics report mistakenly and plausibly that the hundred years of the title is one hundred years of Macondo, the town, or the family, the Buendías, and there has been much fretting as to whether the chronology works. Founded sometime in the nineteenth century (300 years after Sir Francis Drake's attack on Riohacha), crisscrossed by train tracks, telephones, movies, ice factories, and cars, the town prospers and then declines, until it is finally abandoned in the era of air travel and contest prizes.

The family also shows time's changes in the lives its members imagine and create for themselves. The recurring characteristics of the family, Ursula's energy or José Arcadio Buendía's devotion to thought, recur in different worlds. Character is shaped by time: Amaranta Ursula has Ursula's energy, but also a new freedom to enjoy her sexual happiness. Aureliano Babilonia repeats his great-great-great-grandfather's isolation in study, but in the world of the adolescent intellectual, not the world of the patriarchal founder. Having never lived in the heroic world of founding and origins, Aureliano Babilonia does not fall from action to uselessly recondite knowledge already forgotten elsewhere, as his ancestor did. He begins and ends on the margins, in reading, not action. Sometimes for characters, too, time stumbles and stops, as for Fernanda, who brings a timeless rigidity to Macondo, as plausible in the period of the colony or independence as it remains today. The town and the family pass through time, but they are never said to have existed for a hundred years.

The various attempts to work out a chronology for the novel have led to characters of superhuman longevity, and García Márquez has been badgered into conceding that he is not sure whether the time scheme in the novel is exactly one hundred years or not. To date, he has held out against pressure to explain the origins of his title. The principal reason for the difficulty in making "one hundred years" fit Macondo or the Buendías is that the phrase does not apply to them. It applies to the manuscripts of Melquíades, not to the family or the town.

43

Unlike "solitude," which appears promiscuously on every page and is always with us, the phrase "one hundred years" appears in the novel only three times in Spanish, four times in English. The only person or thing in the novel to reach precisely one hundred years of age is the manuscripts of Melquíades. The spectral Melquíades refuses to translate the manuscripts for Aureliano Segundo because *"nadie debe conocer su sentido mientras no hayan cumplido cien años"* ("Nobody must know *their* meaning until *they* have reached a hundred years of age") (177; 262; this crucial sentence is mistranslated in English). Only when they reach one hundred years can the manuscripts be read; later, in another generation, Melquíades is relieved to learn that Aureliano Babilonia has identified the language of the manuscripts, Sanskrit. Only if he knows the language will he be able to read the manuscripts when they become legible in a century (329; 430; the English edition translates *siglo* ["century"] as "one hundred years").

The only other occurrences of the phrase "one hundred years" are in that final reading. Aureliano Babilonia reads the manuscripts written *"con cien años de anticipación"* and finds himself, in a pun on the title, the last of one of *"las estirpes condenadas a cien años de soledad"* ("the races condemned to one hundred years of solitude"). Trapped in the book *One Hundred Years of Solitude,* Aureliano and his ancestors are indeed condemned forever to "one hundred years of solitude." (*"Con cien años de anticipación"* translates as "a hundred years ahead of time," but the literal and un-English "with a hundred years of anticipation" suggests the prevision and the expectancy of the writer, as well as a feature of the novel's temporal structure. In music "anticipation" is the introduction of one note in a new chord before the previous chord has been resolved. In much the same way, the narrator in *One Hundred Years of Solitude* anticipates events before they occur in the narrative or introduces two time frames at once, as in the opening sentence.) What has happened is that the title that has seemed to direct us to external matters, to history and the human condition, finally directs us inward, to the book itself, to the experience of literature, "the best play thing ever invented to make fun of people" (357; 462).

A Pig's Tail, a Pig's Eye

Snakes and Ladders: The Problem of Self-Referentiality

Some readers are genuinely pained by the self-referential conclusion to the world of Macondo. They had expected a meaningful resolution to a world in which they had been immersed; they do not expect to be directed to the center of the onion. Then there rises an anguished and frustrated wail, "If it's just a book, what's the point?" Seemingly more sophisticated critics sniff at the inconsequentiality of fictitious fictions that mirror other fictions, including themselves. Such critics are the meat-and-potatoes (preferably boiled) men of literature. We will leave them chewing on their beef while we respond to the less defensive, genuinely pained reaction that some readers experience with that ending. Why does García Márquez end it that way, why does he do that to his trusting, defenseless reader? Two general observations may console the disconsolate. First, self-referentiality does not invalidate what a text tells us about its subjects, history, life, and time, love, sex, and politics, war, grief, and memory. Quite the contrary: its status as a text is the only thing that makes it possible for it to tell us anything at all. Secondly, instead of subtracting significance from the novel's ostensible subjects, self-referentiality adds still another subject to the text: literary activity itself. The text that points to its own fictitiousness makes one more point than the text that does not: the additional point that it is a fiction. If literature is supposed to enable us to see what we have not seen before, *One Hundred Years of Solitude* makes us more conscious of how peculiar an activity reading is.

There are also consolations more specific to this novel. The absolute value of writing is one of the great subjects of *One Hundred Years of Solitude*. So is truth. The novel marks the absolute value of writing with an antithetical pair of episodes: the insomnia plague and the banana massacre. The insomnia plague begins by attacking memory, and it will end by destroying the significations of words and the values of letters. The insomnia plague, wakefulness without power, produces consciousness without memory and so without self-consciousness. The result is a people lost to themselves, their culture, their language. The insomnia plague is a fantastic emblem: an event so evidently impossible that it nags us until we tease out what it is an emblem of.

Toward the end of the fiction appears its stylistic antithesis: the accurate recounting of the massacre of striking banana workers. If the first episode shows us the danger of losing the reality with the words, the second shows us the actual loss of a reality by official erasure, a reality paradoxically restored by this recounting of the erasure. Writing matters. And so does what the writing says. The text marks a difference between the real past and the past "less true but more comforting" invented by the insomniacs, as it does between the massacre at the train station and its denial in the assertion that Macondo is a happy town where no one has died. Although García Márquez's antithesis between the fantastic and the historical can readily be deconstructed (both episodes, the historical and the fantastic, dissolve into fiction in the novel), the text distinguishes between writing that is true and writing that is false. But, interjects the inconsolable, those examples are writing *about* something; this is just writing about itself. There's no *point* to it.

Our final consolation is no consolation: self-referentiality in *One Hundred Years of Solitude* is part of the novel's playfulness, a playfulness not untinged with malice. Self-referentiality problematizes and ironizes the reader's experience. It breaks a contract and makes the reader feel like an idiot for investing his emotions in the narrative—so you thought this was all *true*? To appreciate the joke on himself (and on Aureliano Babilonia), the reader has to be willing to renounce the fullness of romantic identification. If the reader renounces, he gains, like one of Henry James's protagonists, a fine superiority of perception that is at once aesthetic, moral, ironic, and slightly malicious.

Can there be any comfort in the fact that García Márquez has already anticipated our outrage through another medium? The reader who now yelps at the pinch of fictitiousness had laughed at the inhabitants of Macondo who are infuriated by a similar fraud. They tear up the movie seats when a character, dead and buried in one film, for whom they had wept real tears, reappears in another as an Arab. Bruno Crespi explains that the "cinema was a machine of illusions that did not merit the emotional outbursts of the audience," and the audience abandons the movies "considering that they already had too many troubles of their own to weep over the acted-out misfortunes of imaginary beings" (211; 300). If it's only a movie, what's the point?

Critics often speak of the novel as if it were entirely "about" time or repetition. Or they speak of it as a representation of a "real," "historical" world, entirely forgetful of the literary twist of its conclusion. Or they make literary self-consciousness the whole story, forgetful that we would care very little about the self-referentiality of the fiction if the other things that the novel is about were not important or interesting to us. As in the great bourgeois novels of the nineteenth century, as in Dickens, Balzac, or Flaubert, *One Hundred Years of Solitude* is equally interested in the personal, the social, the political, and the literary. The strength of the novel derives from how fully achieved it is at each level, and the beauty from the precision of its rendering.

THE BABY AND THE PIG; OR, INCESTUOUS PLOTTING

But what of that pig's tail we dismissed so lightly at the beginning of this section? There are many readers and many readings that take that pig's tail very seriously, and few discussions of the novel fail to make heavy weather of the curse of incest that pursues the family. The pig's tail is the visible sign of incest, and surely incest is a very serious thing. "The tragic destiny of the Buendía family is definitively revealed in the family's final annihilation by an act of incest. . . . [Incest] is a curse that condemns the entire line of the Buendías to eternal solitude."[6]

Incest, the pig's tail, and destruction come very close together in those last few pages, as if Macondo's destruction were indeed called down by the incest and its sign. Incest becomes an important motif from the second chapter, when Ursula begins to fret about pigs' tails. When incest finally occurs (and it is a long time coming in spite of all the heavy breathing as Amaranta murmurs dissuasives in her nephew's ear), it generates the pig's tail. Melquíades's manuscripts assure us that Sir Francis Drake attacked Riohacha so that Amaranta Ursula, Aureliano Babilonia, and incest could engender the mythological animal (that is, the child with a pig's tail) that was to bring the line to an end. Almost as soon as that causal link is established, the biblical hurricane levels Macondo.

The author's own first account of his novel also pulls on the pig's tail. Even though the modern author has been murdered by his text and has no standing in interpretation, there are still a few readers who suspect that he may know something they don't, or that he has an inside track on the text, or that he can at least provide a clue as to an interesting place to look. Something is up with that pig's tail, that curly corkscrew pretending to be a plot twist, and something is up with incest, or intelligent critics would not be seduced into a belief in the cyclonic properties of incestuous relations. Incest must be the plot line that holds the novel together, and the pig's tail its sign. So indeed it is, but the line twists into parody. If the critic clings to incest as the explanation for Macondo's fate, he ends up grasping—a pig's tail.

As in other imaginative elaborations of reality in *One Hundred Years of Solitude,* the pig's tail has a firm, even scientific basis in reality. In biological terms, the pig's tail results from what is called the "founder effect": a population with a limited number of founders immediately becomes genetically distinct relative to the larger population pool from which the founders come. A distinctive recessive gene carried by one of the founders passes on as a heterozygote until it manifests itself in a homozygote offspring, who inherits defective genes from both parents. Genes for six-fingered dwarfism, Huntington's chorea, tyrosinemia, and osteodontal dysplasia have all been traced in isolated populations to named founders: Samuel King, Miss Cundick, Louis Gagné and his wife Marie Michel, and one Arnold. Tyrosinemia is fatal to infants, Huntington's chorea to adults, and osteodontal dysplasia, in which one's teeth fall out at age twenty, might as well be (the unchewed life, like the unexamined one, being scarcely worth living). The Buendía defect, attested as a possible human defect but not otherwise traced to the founder effect, belongs in the harmless category of six-fingered dwarfism.[7] It is, however, less disfiguring and less conspicuous than dwarfism. If one had to have a genetic defect from the founder effect, a pig's tail would be among the more benign from which to choose.

Where the manifestation of the pig's tail in Macondo differs from other examples of the founder effect is that no inbreeding takes place in Macondo, until Amaranta Ursula and Aureliano Babilonia. The inbreeding that made José Arcadio Buendía or Ursula Iguarán a carrier of a pig's tail gene occurred not in Macondo but in that other, nameless town in the foothills. As other critics have pointed out, Macondo is not a site of origin. Everything that happens there has already happened elsewhere (including the birth of a child with a pig's tail). "Deferred" until the end of the novel, the pig's tail gene is always already there for Macondo. In a community as isolated as Macondo seems to be, its inhabitants are less remarkable for their incestuous passions than for their self-restraint over so many generations.

A pig's tail is biological. Incest is social or, more precisely, asocial, while incestuous desire is natural, sexual, and unavoidable. As Jocasta says soothingly to Oedipus, "How many men have slept in dreams with their mothers!" Particularly intense bonds between mothers or maternal figures and sons are a Hispanic cultural characteristic, but they are not exclusively Hispanic. My four-year-old son has promised to marry me again [sic] when he grows up, perhaps because his four-year-old girlfriend is threatening to marry her daddy *and* her mommy instead of him. The difference between desire and consummation matters. Replicating the conflict acted out by characters in the novel, critics divide along sexual lines in their attitudes toward the final incestuous consummation.

Male critics tend to respond warmly to the liberating possibilities of incest, the end of generations of frustrated desire. They embrace as unambiguously positive the passionate abandon of that final couple who engender the only child conceived in love in a century (not "a hundred years" but the word *century* applies to the baby as well as to the manuscript). In a delightful essay, "Las formas de hacer el amor en *Cien años de soledad*" (loosely translated, "How they make love in *One Hundred Years of Solitude*"), Gustavo Álvarez Gardeazábal even suggested that the flight from incest is a flight from happiness.[8] And while he certainly had other reasons to write about García Márquez and his "demons," it is difficult not to remember that Vargas Llosa was the future author of *Aunt Julia and the Scriptwriter*.

Female critics tend to be more censorious. They observe severely that the abandonment of that last couple to incest and sensuality enacts the warnings of Freud in *Civilization and Its Discontents*. When the double taboos of incest and adultery are breached, the civilization of Macondo, or at least of the House of the Buendías, collapses. Aureliano stops reading, and Amaranta Ursula stops holding off the ants. The incest taboo may not be fun, but the text seems to suggest that it is necessary. Civilization requires the control of passion, and one uncontrolled passion leads to another, as the last child falls victim to his father's passionate abandonment. Not unlike the male characters in the fiction, male critics seem prepared to risk civilization for the sake of incest with one's aunt. Like the mothers and the aunts charged with preventing incest, who hold off their cousins and their nephews and their sons, female critics seem more committed to the value of preserving civilization. At any rate, if it is incest that brings the world of the book to an end, it is to the female characters that we owe the lengthy deferral of that ending.

This quarrel between male and female critics, between desire and order, need not be resolved here, since it will remain in negotiation in life, as it is in the novel, until our species falls silent or the book ends. Not even the sternest upholder of the incest taboo is inclined to scold the consummators, Amaranta Ursula and Aureliano Babilonia, or to suggest that they should restrain themselves. Their happiness is too harmless, too complete, too brief. As to those critics most scornful of Ursula and her incest taboo, even they would probably find incest less congenial, at least in print, if José Arcadio Buendía raped Amaranta or Aureliano Segundo Meme, the most frequent form of incest. Like the pig's tail among genetic defects, the form of incest García Márquez selects is, in its psychological dimension, entirely benign.

In the social dimension, however, the text deprecates the conditions that make incest possible. Family traditions are broken: Amaranta Ursula and Aureliano do not remember Ursula's warnings about the pig's tail. Connections to others in the community, outside the family, are absent. Nostalgia and the past determine desire, as in Amaranta Ursula's irrational return to Macondo or Aureliano's equally irrational, passive inability to leave. More generally, incest suggests an inward turning of this family, this town, this place. The absence of solidarity with others inhibits social change; the insularity of the strong family unit, when it fails to reach outside itself, brings the family to an ironic end inside itself. Thus allegorized, incest becomes the social equivalent of solitude. A physical act, incest turns into an extended metaphor.

But metaphor is not plot. When the looming doom finally descends plump on the characters, it has no effect at all, good or bad. Other, concurrent events cause the incestuous (and adulterous) couple considerable distress, dismay, and enlightenment—Amaranta Ursula's death, the death of the child, and the child's consumption by ants. But there is no indication that Amaranta Ursula dies because the child has a pig's tail, because she committed incest, or even because she committed adultery. Nor does the narrator use the pig's tail to illuminate Aureliano Babilonia and to open the manuscripts. To establish an unbreakable link between the fate of the Buendías, incest, and the pig's tail, Aureliano need only have remembered something Ursula said in her dotage, or the pig's tail might have figured in the epigraph. Those easy alternatives were rejected. The link between fate, incest, and the pig's tail is deferred to the manuscript: it is established only in reading, not in reality.

Making incest the cause of Macondo's destruction, the explanation for its fate, also creates a reality problem. Genetic defects occur. But how can incest destroy a town? If incest caused towns to be swept away, the whole planet would be aswirl with rubble.

Many things happen in Macondo that happen only in the other world of belief or imagination, but the destruction of Macondo is not a flying carpet or a vanishing Armenian. For Macondo's fate to interest us, it has to be meaningful. Its terms must make sense outside the novel, as well as inside the novel. Every other death in the novel makes such sense; it is reasonable to expect the same from the death of the town. But if we make incest the cause of Macondo's destruction, we are stating something inane relative to the world we live in. We trivialize the action as action, and we miss the specifically literary point that there is, indeed, a difference between reading and "reality," even when all we know of reality is what we have read.

What does destroy Macondo then? The cause depends on the code. At the narrative or reality level, it just happens. That sad little fact is much more serious and less reparable than the founding family's fatal vocation for incest. After the banana company departs, one natural disaster succeeds another: endless rains, interminable drought, and finally a strong wind (as in Vallejo and Asturias). Tired, depleted, forgetful of its past—Macondo is thousands of towns. Then a hurricane smashes up the remnants. Such things happen annually in the Caribbean (and the Pacific and the Bay of Bengal), and they are no one's fault and no one's fate, except as an accident of geography. Marta Morello-Frosch, reading another code, has suggested that it is the absence of historical consciousness that destroys the Buendías and Macondo, but it is difficult to see how historical consciousness can inhibit natural disasters.[9] Other indomitable inhabitants may rebuild (as they do over the San Andreas fault and on the slopes of Vesuvius) the Macondo predicted by Melquíades, "a luminous city with great glass houses where there was no trace remaining of the race of Buendías" (59; 130), but the novel ends before they do.

So if Macondo is destroyed because it is destroyed, why bother

A Pig's Tail, a Pig's Eye

with this incestuous red herring? It is all a matter of putting your incest in the right code. In the literary code where the novel plays with its own textuality, incest brings Macondo to a full stop and puts a period to the Buendías.

Incest (followed by self-discovery) brings down Macondo because incest, followed by self-discovery, brings down the protagonist in the plot structure being parodied, the most venerable plot in the Western tradition, *Oedipus Tyrannos*. Every schoolchild (including Amaranta Ursula and Aureliano) knows that Oedipus does all that he can to avoid killing his father and marrying his mother, and "just because of [his] very efforts to avoid [that fate, he] ended by doing so." Everybody also knows that Oedipus is destroyed not by incest but by its discovery. His full self-recognition achieved after the death of Jocasta, Oedipus's incest conveniently displaces the greater guilt of his patricide. Save for the innocence and ignorance of Amaranta Ursula's death, Aureliano Babilonia's situation reproduces Oedipus's. Aureliano Babilonia discovers who he really is after the death/departure of his wife; he too is destroyed by the act of self-discovery and must bear his burden of self-recognition forever. But his "forever" is only a text's, not reality's.

Parody stings in the differences. Aureliano's adventure shows not Sophocles's weighty discovery of meaning through action, but the lighter, less fraught construction of meaning by a text. Instead of mediating man's relation to the dim justice of the gods, our hero discovers that he is only a character in someone else's writings, and we know the writer is no more real than he is. The very insignificance of the incestuous act to the outcome of *One Hundred Years of Solitude* underscores the emptying of meaning, while the ludicrous pig's tail puts our human fondness for the portentous in a modern place.[10] What we lose as significance, however, we regain as power: García Márquez's Sophoclean parody also shows us literature in the act of transforming reality and creating meaning where there was none before.

As Aureliano begins to read, the novel we have just read begins to undergo some changes. It gains in pathos as we learn for the first time that the encyclicals chanted to Arcadio by Melquíades were the prediction of Arcadio's death. It gains in gritty realism as the love affair of the butterflies, Meme and Mauricio, takes a sour turn.[11] The manuscript's reinterpretation of reality peaks when it changes "the irremediable wearing of the axle," the too simple, too irreversible ravages of time, into the single line of a purposive narrative that extends from Sir Francis Drake to a mythological animal. Reading is interpretation, and reinterpretation, as those shifts make clear.

When Aureliano Babilonia begins to read the manuscripts of Melquíades, he discovers that his child with a pig's tail is "the mythological animal that was to bring the line to an end" (383; 492). When the child is born, Aureliano Babilonia has not an inkling of that tremendous significance. The child is healthy and vigorous, with the tail of a pig on his little bottom. He is to be named Aureliano, not Rodrigo, and his ambitious father expects him to win 32 wars. That child is eaten by ants, and he does not appear in the manuscripts. In the manuscript there is no child, there is only the "mythological animal." The literary language transforms the experience utterly. It makes the actual lived experience of Amaranta Ursula, Aureliano, and their child entirely unrecognizable. Reality, the lived experience of a couple and their child, has been transformed and given a significance that, on its own, reality lacks. The personal past has been distorted, and the surviving participant is now able to imbue his disastrous experience with weighty, and perhaps consoling, meanings.

But surely this transformation is a little excessive, the sort of thing one could get away with only in a book? "Mythological animal," forsooth, for a baby with a pig's tail? Give me a break—or a minotaur, a chimera, a uruborus biting its tail. Give me an iguana! (Women do give birth to iguanas every now and then in the *National Enquirer*, dateline remote places like Macondo.) But don't call a pig-tailed baby a "mythological animal" unless you want me to suspect that Melquíades is Blacamán the Good's brother or a magnet-peddling gypsy, hawking his ingots as the eighth wonder of the learned alchemists of Macedonia. The child differed physically from other children, but the difference of words is infinitely greater than the physical difference. Even though we can no longer believe our myths, we still make them.

A Pig's Tail, a Pig's Eye

"Literally," when Aureliano reads the manuscript, that poor child has become a "mythological animal." He was transformed into myth by Ursula before he existed. He was a story before he was born, part of a traditional family knowledge, passed from generation to generation. Now, through the manuscript, Aureliano Babilonia recovers the myth realized only through that child. Now the child is only a key that opens another story that is only partly his, in which he is only the victimized, climactic character. His is not even a walk-on part, for he is dragged offstage before he has the opportunity to utter a line.

7

A Biographical Reading

I wanted only to give a poetic permanence to the world of my childhood. . . .

While his novel was in progress, García Márquez thought for a time that the last Aureliano committed suicide. As it turned out, he was mistaken. Instead of dying in despair by his own hand (like Jocasta), Aureliano perishes permanently with his eyes open, reading. He is caught in "the last that remained of a past whose annihilation had not taken place because it was still in a process of annihilation, consuming itself from within, ending at every moment but never ending its ending" (371; 478).

Verging always on its own ending, that splendid sentence refers to Macondo, yet it also describes any novel verging on its own ending, especially this novel that ends poised before the last sentence of its own manuscript. It also describes the personal past, always already dead and always dying, but never entirely dead until the death of the last person who remembers. Then it is annihilated indeed. Depending on the referent we choose, the sentence changes meanings, as does the novel itself. Different codes shimmer into one another, and if using the wrong code (social realism for incest, for example) creates comic difficulties, the codes themselves blend, soften, and unite a thousand ways.

A Biographical Reading

For very good reasons, García Márquez's critics have neglected the autobiographical code that the author perversely favors.[1] In the first place, the autobiographical references are too obvious: with a character named Gabriel Márquez going off to write in Paris and the web of connections to the author's earlier writings and childhood, the autobiographical code looks too much like unmediated source material. The bits of biographical data woven into the text have the same status as historical, scientific, and literary allusions, but they do not make as clear a picture as the other kinds of data do. They remain bits of data. Second, Vargas Llosa has surely said all that needs to be said on so romantic a topic. Finally, the novel lacks the introspective cast we associate with autobiographical fiction. If the novel is "about" any real persons or places, it is about the author's grandparents and town, his friends and his wife, not himself. Yet as Severo Sarduy observed, the novel is also conspicuously "about" its own production.

One Hundred Years of Solitude turns autobiographical encoding into both literary and political codes, as the code of writing/reading displaces living. The novel assumes our post–eighteenth-century fascination with the character or "self" of the author and shows us that self disappearing into the object it makes, the book, the world of the book. The more successful the author's expression or self-expression, the more invisible is the "real" self (whatever that is for any of us) whose obsessions, experiences, and skills brought the work into being. The work submerges its origins, as in "The Last Voyage of the Ghost Ship" the townsfolk see only the great ghostly ocean liner, not the young man who guides it to shore. The autobiographical code leaves its traces everywhere in the novel—on its structure, in its names. It also crystallizes certain ambiguities and illuminates certain puzzles; but it does so only when the autobiography of the author is transmuted into the biography of the book.

No one doubts that at one level the history of Macondo charts the (cultural) transit from childhood to adulthood. Macondo, or José Arcadio Buendía, moves from Renaissance credulity to enlightenment skepticism to backwater of the industrial revolution. In Western culture's view of itself, this triumphant progress is taken to mark man's emergence from darkness into the light and power of maturity. Lamented by poets, the magic of childhood fades, and with it childhood's credulity and powerlessness. (Treating magic realism literally, several critics have found it damaging to Macondo or insufficient: magic compensates for the lack of science, as childhood's wonder compensates for lack of knowledge. If one settles for magic or permanent childhood, however, one has settled for the serene peaceful state of being a fool among knaves, and one is in deep trouble.) Unfortunately for Macondo, it arrives at adulthood in the pupilage of foreigners. A rebellious Macondo is shot down at the train station and then collapses into senescence. Insofar as the narrative is skeptical of "progress," it is skeptical of progress imposed from outside. When the community is not empowered and real power remains lodged far away, the community decays.

In that senescence the last Aureliano (Babilonia) grows up, just as García Márquez saw the light in an Aracataca whose glories had faded and whose prosperity had passed. Yet just when the autobiographical references begin unmistakably to cluster (no one can miss "Gabriel Márquez," who prompts the search for the rest), the autobiographical structure seems to break down. Aracataca has been destroyed by no cyclones. What has befallen Aracataca, "the world of my childhood," is that it has been made into a book. The autobiographical code passes without a break into the code of the writer.

There is a deep—and fiendish?—glee in the narrative voice as the text sweeps toward its end. As Aureliano reads, oblivious to everything save the manuscript, the narrator tears the doors from the hinges and spins Macondo into a "fearful whirlwind of dust and rubble." Aureliano just reads on (383; 492). It is all very reminiscent of those wonderful old ads for the *Philadelphia Bulletin*. A trainload of commuters is about to be overtaken by some terrible disaster, and one alert, frantic soul is trying desperately to arouse them to save themselves. Alas, no one raises his eyes from his paper, for "in Philadelphia, nearly everybody reads the *Bulletin*." From the energy and the glee with which the narrator sweeps Macondo away, many critics have derived a positive, political reading for the novel's conclusion. Others, more attached to the world being swept away, so finally and so brutally, detest or deplore the hopelessness of that spectacular finale. It must not end like this, especially when there is no promise of anything else to come. There is a persuasive political reading of this duality, but there is an almost equally persuasive biographical reading; both depend on a single word, *Rodrigo*.

If the ending of *One Hundred Years of Solitude* celebrates the final "translation" of *La casa* into a book, that ending has also to lament the passing of the world thus translated. If the author has finally succeeded in giving "a poetic permanence to the world of my childhood," his success signals both the death of that world and his separation from the project of making a book about it. The energy with which that world is swept away suggests not only the release of an author as he writes himself out of a life-consuming fiction, but also a determined collaboration with necessity. All of the past is "unrepeatable since time immemorial and forevermore."

There is always ambivalence in such a moment, and for García Márquez there is also literary humor. The birth of *One Hundred Years of Solitude* is the death of the author, all of them. Melquíades, that up-to-date gypsy, begins to write only after he has already died once, and as his text begins to find its reader, he reaffirms "the death of the author." "I died of fever on the sands of Singapore" are Melquíades's last words at his last appearance, when he knows that the language of his text has been identified (329; 431). When Aureliano Segundo tried to decipher the manuscripts so long ago, Melquíades was "no more than forty years old"—like an invisible García Márquez—and when he departs, the magic room becomes vulnerable to creatures it is difficult for a critic not to identify as critics: "dust, heat, termites, red ants, and moths, who would turn the wisdom of the parchments into sawdust" (176; 261; 329; 431; the English translation "under forty years of age" misses the joke). Aureliano survives the end by becoming a reader, not an author.

The book emerges (finishes) through the translation of a manuscript that concentrates "a century of daily episodes in such a way that they coexisted in one instant" (382; 491). That puzzling feature must be assimilable in some way to the novel, which is and is not the manuscript. (The manuscript is in two codes and Sanskrit; the novel is in Spanish. A persuasive account makes the novel a translated, edited version of the manuscript, with Gabriel Márquez, now in Paris, the probable, future editor.) Little whirlpools of simultaneous times punctuate *One Hundred Years of Solitude,* but most of the text is linear and sequential, with no attempt to evoke simultaneity. If it were otherwise, we could not read it. Where simultaneous coexistence flourishes is in a writer's mind before he succeeds in translating images and ideas into words and sentences. Writing "translates" simultaneity into linearity. In the code of literary biography, Melquíades's manuscript represents the state from which the book must emerge in order to be read, not only as writing to be printed but also as writing written. Like that drawerful of memoranda, it is a state of the text we never see.

Almost as soon as the novel appeared, García Márquez developed an unsettling habit of describing his life in terms of his novel. He assured interviewer after interviewer that he should have been a magician rather than a novelist. Such malicious mischief continues outside the novel, the essential dialectic of the novel's technique. As Edwin Williamson put it, the novel is "predicated upon a dialectic that opposes the experiences of the world *inside* the fiction to that which lies *outside* it."[2] When bizarre events happen inside the fiction, they force us to judge or naturalize them by reference to our experience or knowledge of life, literature, and history outside the fiction (as, for example, in the reading of the simultaneity of Melquíades's manuscripts). When the real author inserts himself into the text from outside the novel, he confuses matters even more hopelessly. One of the testier quarrels between fiction and reality took place over the book that Gabriel Márquez takes to Paris. In an early commentary on the novel, Tzvetan Todorov seized upon the fact that Gabriel Márquez took Rabelais to Paris with him, while Gabriel *García* Márquez raged back that that was a trick to catch critics—he *really* took Defoe's *Journal of the Plague Year.* He? Which he? How does "he" know, and what on earth does "really" mean in such a context? But who took what? *You* figure it out; this one is beyond me.

Autobiographical references occur throughout the novel, but they cluster and become more obtrusive toward the end. It is in the last generation that Aureliano meets the "four friends," Álvaro, Germán, Alfonso, and Gabriel, clustered around the wise Catalan. These characters correspond to the "Grupo de Barranquilla"—Álvaro Cepeda Samudio, Alfonso Fuenmayor, Germán Vargas, and Gabriel García Márquez—clustered around the Catalan Ramón Vinyes. García Márquez wrote columns for *El Heraldo* on Vinyes both when Vinyes left Barranquilla and when he died in Barcelona. Gabriel has a stealthy girlfriend with Egyptian looks named Mercedes, like the wife of García Márquez, Mercedes Barcha. Gabriel Márquez is a descendant of Col. Gerineldo Márquez, comrade-in-arms of Col. Aureliano Buendía, much as García Márquez is a descendant of Col. Nicolás Márquez, comrade-in-arms of Rafael Uribe Uribe, the model for the legendary Col. Aureliano Buendía.

Most of the overt autobiographical references are placed at the margins of the fiction. The Márquezes are friends of the Buendías, and they fail even to marry into the family. The four friends and Mercedes disappear. The wise Catalan dies far away. The exceptions are the names Iguarán and Cotes, the family names of García Márquez's grandmother, the names of Amaranta Ursula's unborn children, Rodrigo and Gonzalo, and the name the last child is almost given, Rodrigo. That Ursula should bear the patronymic of the grandmother to whom García Márquez has always attributed the narrative tone of the novel seems entirely appropriate. That imperturbable, authoritative teller of impossible tales gives more than her name to the matriarchal interpreter of the family. Ursula Iguarán, descendant of Tranquilina (the author's grandmother's first name), is trusted by critics as if she were their own grandmother and would not lie or be mistaken. They rarely doubt her, even when they dislike her and accuse her of overbearing rigidity. Iguarán and Cotes support and sustain the fiction over long stretches, but the children are focused much more narrowly. They appear only at the end, at the crucial point where the line will continue or be broken.

Amaranta Ursula wants to name her children Rodrigo and Gonzalo, the names of García Márquez's children. When her first son is born, she says immediately, "He's a real cannibal. . . . We'll name him Rodrigo" (378; 487). García Márquez's first son, born in 1959, is Rodrigo. Fortunately, Aureliano overrules his spouse, and it is not Rodrigo but an Aureliano who is eaten by ants.

All of this is familiar enough, and unmistakable. García Márquez has often said that the novel is full of coded asides to and about his friends and relations. The question is whether the abortive naming of Rodrigo is just cute and gratuitous or whether it can be fitted into a code and made to mean something. Silly question: of course it can be made to mean something. There is even a traditional metaphor that identifies books and babies, pregnancy and authorship, the length of gestation and the painful labor of delivery.

In many traditional cultures, there is one event that signifies manhood: the birth of one's first son. "Now you really are a man," Pilar Ternera tells José Arcadio when she discovers she is pregnant by him (38; 104). Making a baby, making a book: if the last character born is almost named for García Márquez's first son, the last words of the book name his book.

It is a great liberation, but it is also the death of a past, and no one knows what lies beyond it. If Aureliano Babilonia is trapped in that last line, García Márquez is released by it. Writing Aureliano reading his novel into the novel, he writes himself out. When he completes that mission, he himself disappears. "Now they'll see who I am," he said in his new man's voice, the adolescent who beaches the great, ghostly ocean liner that only he has ever been able to see in "The Last Voyage of the Ghost Ship." Like the boy who strands the great dead ocean liner, our narrator has beached a past and ghostly reality for all the world to see. When he found the galleon, the galleon that "really" derives from a sunken transatlantic liner in Hemingway, García Márquez knew that his book was going to live. " 'Now they're going to see who I am,' she said when she saw that her son was going to live" (173; 257). The speaker is Ursula, when her son Aureliano, the colonel, recovers after his failed suicide. But as the boy and Ursula forget (and García Márquez does not forget), what "they" see is the ocean liner, Aureliano, Macondo, and never "who I am."

8

A Political Reading

There is also a political reading carried by the name Rodrigo. Critics quarreling about the implications of the ending are often motivated by the discrepancy they perceive between the view of the human condition articulated in *One Hundred Years of Solitude* and the political convictions of the author. Optimistic revolutionary, faithful friend of Fidel, illusionless prophet of the fate of Salvador Allende, García Márquez cannot have told the distressingly hopeless version of Latin American history that he seems to have told.[1] That sweeping away of Macondo at the end, that breathless and joyous reduction of the past to a silent, dispersed manuscript, must augur the advent of a new world, a world where races are no longer condemned to a hundred years of solitude, where, as García Márquez said in his Nobel Prize acceptance speech, they have a second chance. It must be. But critics such as Donald Shaw have found no trace of any promise of a new world about to be born. The patterned repetitions of the novel do not augur well for new beginnings, and progress seems to lead only to an irreversible decline. How can a revolutionary socialist have so little confidence in the past, in history, and so little hope for the future? Rodrigo tells us what we need to know.

A Political Reading

When Amaranta Ursula names Rodrigo, she names more than the author's first son. She also points to the year in which that son was born: 1959, an important year to García Márquez for both biographical and political reasons. It was the year his first son was born in August, but it was a year that had begun, in January, with the triumphant entry of Fidel's *guerrilleros* into Havana. It was the year that saw the triumph of a Latin American revolution that would shape revolutionary hopes and aspirations for more than two decades. Nor was that revolution remote to García Márquez. He made his way to Havana that year, and for several years thereafter, in Bogotá and New York, he represented Prensa Latina, the Cuban news agency that was one voice of the revolution. While the novel articulates no overt, explicit hope for a new world on revolutionary principles when Macondo is blown away, such a hope seems unmistakably implicit in the cipher Rodrigo, who sees light in February.

Many critics have commented that Amaranta Ursula's introducing a new name is an attempt to change the direction of history, to move the family into a new world. That attempt is rejected by Aureliano, who wants only to make the old version come out better. (He overrules her with sweeping, unhesitating masculine authority so as to continue an old model of gender relations as well.) Amaranta Ursula's failure to create a new name marks Macondo's and the Buendías' failure to start over again, and Macondo and the Buendías, representing the past, are condemned to destruction with no sign of promise. That reading is coherent and fundamentally correct, but it leaves out the encoding of political promise, just as it leaves out Melquíades's promise of glass houses. "Rodrigo" 's natal year marks the direction Macondo does not take and, perhaps, the destruction of solitude.

The allusion made through Rodrigo is so cryptic as to suggest a critical artifact. Only those close to García Márquez would recognize the name (before success made his private life a quarry), and they would not make the connection to the year. (No one ever remembers the birth dates of other people's children.) It is also based on pure coincidence, the accident of a natal year. Still, accidents may be useful, and "Rodrigo" is not the only example of a cryptic allusion to the revolutionary politics of the 1960s. Such encoding is typical of García Márquez's management of references to his own present in *One Hundred Years of Solitude*.

For those who can recognize them, the references are there. The revolutionary sympathizer who knows nothing of Rodrigo will not miss *Moncada*. The Colombian political activist, right or left, will recognize Victorio Medina. Those names, like the revolutionary transformation of Latin America, glint in the text as sparks of hope relative to a conflagration that has not yet occurred—not in 1967, nor in 1990—but that seemed considerably closer in 1966 than it seems now.

By encoding his references to the future-present, García Márquez avoids making his novel an expression of simple political desire. As a general matter, it is fair, if unkind, to say that García Márquez's political ideology is simple, much too simple. Since the period of the Terror in the French Revolution, revolutionary socialists have sought political solutions to economic problems that cannot be solved *without* politics but are only made worse by politics alone. Only politics can solve problems of distribution, but politics makes a hash of production. It is also fair to say that García Márquez's grasp of political dynamics and the realities of political power makes a mockery of the more "complex" bourgeois ideologies that dismiss his as too simple.[2]

In *One Hundred Years of Solitude*, the choice of a revolutionary politics begins as an easy choice of liberalism and becomes progressively harder, more radical, and more dangerous. The difficulty, ambivalence, and danger of that choice are related through the history of Col. Aureliano Buendía. So powerfully are they represented that it is possible for a reader to be persuaded that counterrevolution is preferable and to opt for the status quo. Readers may even suppose that the author is skeptical of all politics, or they may argue that the author's art subverts his ideology. Obviously enough, such positions will be argued most strenuously by those who, in their own politics, oppose revolutionary solutions. Authors can think what they will, but no critic tolerates a position he finds repulsive in a text he likes. The author may go hang or eat grass, but the critic will "save" the text.

A Political Reading

One Hundred Years of Solitude permits contradictory political readings for two principal reasons. It represents the revolutionary choice as a hard one in human terms. And it represents the past, what we have known and tried, as narrative, while the future, what we hope for, is represented only as allusion, in isolated, specific details. Such a management of politics corresponds, appropriately enough, to the novel's management of history.

The best studies of the historical bases of the novel are Lucila Mena's, but those studies are hampered by a failure to recognize the freedom García Márquez takes with history. Because Mena began by studying the banana strike, she seems to have assumed that that episode was typical of his management of history and that his treatment of historical events was therefore uniform. But García Márquez plays with history as he plays with anecdote, literature, and biography. Sometimes, as in his reconstruction of the massacre at the Ciénaga train station in 1928, the labor unrest that preceded it, and the erasure that followed, he is scrupulously accurate. But at other times, he exercises what used to be called poetic license and could be called "creative anachronism."

Instead of cleaving to a realistic, historical time frame, he bends historical references as he bends realistic geography, so that Macondo is now Ciénaga, now Aracataca. For poetic purposes, he takes shocking liberties with "real" history and rejects the historian's condition, captive to the truths of a foolish world. Nor is he interested only in the nostalgic reconstruction of the career of his grandfather's commander-in-chief, Gen. Rafael Uribe Uribe. He tells a whole story of Colombia's violent politics and connects that story, however lightly, to the great revolutionary movements of his own time. There is no reason for him to adhere to historical chronology.

That García Márquez intends not to be bound by the rigid and useful frames of the historical novel is established by the opening of the fiction. There he establishes a slippery present in a slippery place. One of the fundamental conventions of reading is that a writing is set in the present unless another date is indicated. Similarly, the reader's solipsism takes the place of the reading to be his own nation, country, and race until another place is established by the fiction. To that end, the historical novel always tactfully slips in a date, while the realistic novel enumerates objects whose material coherence establishes the present of the fiction. But *One Hundred Years of Solitude* does not begin in *Buddenbrooks*'s "our year of grace 1835," and the incoherent objects of its first pages estrange the fiction's present from the present of the modern urban reader.

At first, and for some time, the reader of *One Hundred Years of Solitude* feels dislocated, both in space and time. Where is this place so isolated that the people, visited by gypsies, do not know that the world is round? Where is this place? It has a name, Macondo, that is not much help. It has firing squads, mules, goats, and gypsies with magical magnets; it has astrolabes, ice, and fifteenth-century skeletons in armor. The reader is halfway through the first chapter before a name is offered that might enable the Colombian, Venezuelan, or other-Caribbean reader to identify the place: Riohacha.

If the reader is not Colombian or Venezuelan or Veracruzano, Riohacha is as illuminating a place name as Macondo. Riohacha is not one of the famous cities of Latin America, and besides, it is not the place. The Buendías were never there in the history of the narrative, and the Iguaráns left it some five generations before the founding of Macondo to live in some other, entirely nameless village in the foothills of the mountains where a Don José Arcadio Buendía was already settled. Even the reader who, by some lucky chance of birth or good geography lessons, knows Riohacha, knows no more.

If the reader cannot locate the space, what about the time? When is this place? Here the reader seems to get more help, but the help is contradictory. The reader is quite close to the creation of the world and to Adam's naming of the animals, since the boulders of Macondo's little river resemble "prehistoric eggs" and the "world was so new" that many things were yet unnamed. Yet the adulthood of one whose childhood was spent in this Arcadian, prehistoric landscape already contains firing squads. That childhood also takes place well after the

A Political Reading

fifteenth century, we discover in a few moments, because a fifteenth-century suit of armor has had time to rust and the skeleton inside to calcify—not the work of a moment. Not until the second chapter do we find the strategic date that locates us in the nineteenth century: three hundred years ago, Sir Francis Drake attacked Riohacha. (Sir Francis Drake attacked Riohacha in 1568, bombarding the treasurer's house, and he occupied the town for almost two weeks on his last voyage in 1595.[3])

Meanwhile, the details have violated our hard-won, enlightened, nineteenth-century historical sense. Firing squads abut magical magnets and alchemists. The positivist promise of science—namely, television—collides with Nostradamus as Melquíades proclaims, "Science has eliminated distance. . . . In a short time, man will be able to see what is happening in any place in the world without leaving his own house" (12; 73). By thus unsettling his reader, García Márquez gains (for the same unsettled reader) that remarkable, exuberant sense of having found and entered a wholly new world. The reader cannot pinpoint and pigeonhole Macondo, as the names Aracataca, Ciénaga, Riohacha, Colombia, and "Atlantic Coast" force him to do. Those names take us out of Macondo to another geography that exists on other maps, to parts of a bigger picture. In its dislocations of space and time, Macondo establishes itself as its own world and the only picture.

Paradoxically, however, Macondo does exist on real maps: maps of the banana zone around Aracataca. The reader will find "the real Macondo" if he pursues the massacre of striking banana workers out of the fiction into García Márquez's own source, the exculpatory account of Gen. Carlos Cortés Vargas.[4] Thus subjected to real history, Macondo is a small part of a larger whole. But that real Macondo is not "the" Macondo; it is "a" Macondo that has been supplanted by its fictive elaboration and transmuted from reality into a footnote. Such alchemical transformations continue Williamson's dialectic between what is inside the novel and what is outside.

At the beginning, then, García Márquez establishes an authorial prerogative to mix times even as he sets off on a curving, but generally linear, progressive movement through the nineteenth century into the twentieth. The narrative is always curving back, making loops to catch up to its present, and those loops make free with the passage of time. They go back 300 years to the Renaissance and Sir Francis Drake, 400 years to the fifteenth-century suit of armor, and 2,400 years to Thales, the Greek philosopher of the magnets (640?–546 B.C.). Through the history of Macondo the narrative simultaneously charts the social (and intellectual) development of Western man, saved from darkness by the Arabs (gypsy = Egyptian), and the historical development of Latin America from the conquest to the twentieth century. It also provides an account of one region's experience of political development, colonial exploitation, and decay.

The founding of Macondo recapitulates a specifically Latin American and Colombian history: intrepid explorers find their way over impassable mountains and through impenetrable jungles to found a town and divide the land. In spite of their conviction that they are the first to see this terrain, they are mistaken, as the narrative reminds us at the end of the first paragraph. The skeleton in armor was also mistaken if he thought he was the first. Later, the central government arrives and seeks to exert control through its magistrate and its soldiers but finds itself initially stalemated by the representatives of local authority. That resistance is at first apolitical—the Buendía house is painted white, neither red, the Liberal color, nor blue, the Conservative color. But it is unmistakably the resistance of a powerful local magnate who resents the intrusion of an alternative source of authority.

With the arrival of political and party divisions, Macondo is plunged into the civil wars of the nineteenth century. Typical of Latin American historiography and self-representation, there is little sense of a colonial period. Instead, the narrative makes a great leap from conquest/founding to independence. As several critics have pointed out, the arrival of church and state, followed by the plunge into history's wars, takes place only after Melquíades returns to waken the town from the oblivion and forgetfulness of the insomnia plague. Rescued from an eternal, mindless, wordless present, Macondo discovers the equally dubious pleasures of history. At this point in the narrative the system of references becomes more specifically Colombian, while remaining temporally mixed.

For the most part, as Mena has so well documented, the wars of Col. Aureliano Buendía represent the career of the Liberal general Rafael Uribe Uribe. The description by Moscote, Aurelito's father-in-law, of the difference between Liberals and Conservatives insists quite properly upon the centralist, clerical orientation of nineteenth-century Conservatives and the federalist, anticlerical orientation of nineteenth-century Liberals. Their wars lasted from the 1860s to 1902, and the colonel's almost 20 years of war and 32 lost wars are relatively conservative by the standards of nineteenth-century Colombian warfare.[5] Less plausibly, Mena has suggested the novel ends with the *bogotazo* in 1948.

The *bogotazo* was a three-day riot provoked by the assassination of the Liberal candidate for president, Jorge Eliécer Gaitán. It burned blocks of Bogotá, including the pension in which García Márquez was living, closed down the National University, at which García Márquez was studying, and sent the law student scurrying back to the coast, to Cartagena and then to Barranquilla, to be subverted by literature. From the *bogotazo* dates *la violencia,* "almost twenty years" of civil war that left 250,000 Colombians dead between 1948 and 1964. Indirectly, the *bogotazo* helped make García Márquez a writer rather than a lawyer.

Nor did *la violencia* impede his literary development. The armed conflicts between Liberal and Conservative bands, between civilians and army or police, did not affect the coastal region, and they also provided literary material. As a politician, Gaitán had some significance for García Márquez: it was Gaitán, as a young legislator, who had led the defense of the banana strikers in the banana zone and had demanded investigation of the massacre at Ciénaga. *La violencia* is the background to García Márquez's earlier novels, *In Evil Hour* and *No One Writes to the Colonel,* and it was the major domestic political preoccupation of the author's youth. But for all the connections between García Márquez and *la violencia, One Hundred Years of Soli-*

tude does not end with the beginning of *la violencia,* for the compelling reason that *la violencia* is woven through the account of the colonel's wars. The novel ends neither in 1948, as Mena proposes, nor in 1928, as the author once proposed, "the year I was born." (If it did, it should end with the banana strike, which took place in 1928.) It probably ends in no particular year, but the last year it points to is 1959.[6]

That García Márquez intends his account of the colonel's wars to go beyond even *la violencia* as well as the wars of the nineteenth century and the War of a Thousand Days is marked from the moment Aurelito, now Col. Aureliano Buendía, sets off. He is on his way to join the forces of the revolutionary general Victorio Medina. Like Cortés Vargas, Victor Medina is a historical figure, but he is not a figure out of the nineteenth century; nor was he a revolutionary "general." He was a founder and leader of the ELN (Army of National Liberation), the Colombian guerrilla army that Camilo Torres, the guerrilla priest, joined in 1965.[7]

Torres had been a friend of García Márquez at the university, and he baptized Rodrigo, García Márquez's first son. Son of an aristocratic Colombian family, he became a priest for the people, and his efforts brought him into conflict with the highly conservative Colombian hierarchy. Disciplined by his superiors and removed from his cure, Torres took his vocation for the poor to the field and joined the ELN in July 1965. While García Márquez was writing *One Hundred Years of Solitude,* Torres died in his first encounter with Colombian troops in February 1966. The child who is not Rodrigo dies in a radiant February dawn (381; 490). In a film about Torres's life and death, García Márquez testified to their friendship, but he also maintained that Torres would have done more good had he stayed alive as a priest, rather than dying as a *guerrillero.*

Since the death of Camilo Torres, "liberation theology" has made great strides throughout Latin America; there have been other revolutionary priests—Cardenal in Nicaragua, for example—and there have been many other clerical martyrs to human liberation, such as Archbishop Romero in El Salvador. But Torres led the way in a much more

A Political Reading

hostile time. "Camilo Torres" is a famous name throughout Latin America, too famous for García Márquez to use. "Victor Medina" is not. But just as García Márquez points unmistakably to the banana strike of 1928 by using the names of Cortés Vargas, his secretary, and their decrees, so by using Victor Medina's name, García Márquez points unmistakably, specifically, and perhaps ironically to the guerrilla conflicts of the 1960s and the radicalization of *la violencia*. Victor Medina was less successful than even Col. Aureliano Buendía.

As Minta has pointed out, Col. Aureliano Buendía is initially almost without ideology. He has no interest in the positions of the traditional parties as his father-in-law lays them out, and he chooses armed resistance only in response to the physical brutalities of the Conservative regime: the execution without due process of the homeopathic anarchist Dr. Noguera, the attack on the levitating priest with a soldier's rifle butt, and the murder, also with rifle butts, of a woman bitten by a mad dog. The initial humanitarian bias toward the Liberals soon dissipates as Liberal atrocities surpass Conservative atrocities. When Col. Aureliano Buendía's career ends, he too has traded humanity for ideology. His Conservative opponent Gen. José Raquel Moncada will be more humane and sympathetic than the ostensible hero.

Once the colonel's wars begin, the socioeconomic conflicts of the twentieth century rapidly replace the political conflicts of the nineteenth. José Arcadio, the macho, is usually remembered (fondly) for his huge penis, tattooed all over, and his enviable and envied sexuality. He makes women pay for his sexual favors and gives up that easy life to marry his "little sister," Rebeca. (No incestuous union this, at least no more than the Song of Songs' "my sister, my spouse": Rebeca arrives in Macondo only after José Arcadio has left with the gypsy girl, and her relation to the Buendías remains forever unascertained. Ursula overreacts, and another gap opens between language and action.) A fantasy of machismo, José Arcadio the macho is also the great illegal engrosser of land. He descends from the line of the Montiels and Sabas in García Márquez's earlier fictions of *la violencia*.

During the wars, José Arcadio, "it was said," began "by plowing

73

his own yard and [going] straight ahead into neighboring lands, knocking down fences and buildings with his oxen until he took forcible possession of the best plots of land around. On the peasants whom he had not despoiled because he was not interested in their lands, he levied a contribution *which he collected every Saturday with his hunting dogs and his double-barreled shotgun.* He did not deny it" (114; 190; my italics). As Fuentes pointed out, the Buendías unite the Sartorises and the Snopeses: if Col. Aureliano Buendía is a heroic Sartoris, this aspect of his brother José Arcadio is the acquisitive, unscrupulous Snopes. But José Arcadio encounters a distinctively Colombian violence that Flem Snopes did not meet in Mississippi.

Arcadio, José Arcadio's son by Pilar Ternera, arranges a legal title to the usurped lands in return for José Arcadio's financial support for the Liberal party. The Conservative government also recognizes the legalized usurpation (129; 208). Five sentences after the Conservative government recognizes his title, José Arcadio is murdered in his bedroom one afternoon after he returns from hunting. He has his double-barreled shotgun and a string of rabbits. For a rare moment, the narrator puts on the idiot face of Blacamán the Good to tell his readers that this was a mystery that was never cleared up and that no one could understand why Rebeca should have murdered the man who made her happy. Casting suspicion elsewhere even before he relates the death, our narrator colludes with the silence of the town. Both know that José Arcadio was shot after his weekly rounds by someone taxed or someone dispossessed. Whoever did it, the town and the narrator conspire to prevent official justice with ostentatious ignorance, and they leave suspicion on Rebeca for safekeeping. This is a story of *la violencia,* and it has ties with "Big Mama's Funeral" and "Montiel's Widow."

The colonel is linked with *la violencia* on the other side through his politics and his military action. The colonel's radicalization is manifested by his revision of land titles and the return of the lands usurped by his dead brother to their rightful owners (114. 152–53, 159; 190, 233–34, 240). Such radical reforms drive Liberal property owners to characterize their own armed supporters as bandits and to combine with the Conservative regime to end the war. "Bandits" is the conventional Latin American and Colombian designation for nongovernmental organized violence; the term erases ideological motivation for the "bandits" and their supporters. As to the parties, they erase (or replace) their own ideologies when they abandon their political differences to retain class power. Once the war ends and the colonel retires, the situation of the veterans, waiting endlessly for their pensions, recalls *No One Writes to the Colonel,* set in 1956 (228; 256).

In twentieth-century Colombian history, the National Front, formed in 1957, erased political differences with inimitable panache. Like the judicial determination in the banana strike, one would think García Márquez had invented it had it not actually happened. *La violencia* had stymied even the dictator Rojas Pinilla, who used it to justify taking power in 1953. In 1957 the directorates of the Liberal and Conservative parties agreed to alternate in power, four years a Liberal president, four years a Conservative, and so on, with shared cabinet posts. Each party also agreed to withdraw support from the armed bands carrying on the conflict, an agreement more costly to Liberal bands than to Conservatives. This arrangement was worked out by "the politicians of the parties," the black-frocked lawyers and other hovering functionaries who plague Col. Aureliano Buendía. It gave rise to the caustic popular saying, quoted by the retired Col. Aureliano Buendía, that the only difference between Liberals and Conservatives is that the Liberals go to mass at five o'clock and the Conservatives at eight (228; 319).

Other twentieth-century episodes in the colonel's ostensibly nineteenth-century career implicate foreigners in the national violence. A shout leads to the assassination of his 17 sons: "One of these days . . . I'm going to arm my boys so we can get rid of these shitty gringos" (224; 316). "*Un día de estos*" ("One of these days") is the title of one of García Márquez's stories of *la violencia.* "Gringos" is us, U.S. citizens, at home and abroad. The colonel's shout is provoked by the ugliest atrocity in the novel. One of the new policemen protecting the gringos' interests cuts a child to pieces with a machete and decapitates the boy's grandfather. The consequence is the systematic extermination of those potential subversives, the colonel's sons, by assailants the government is unable to identify. Such death squads, often trained by the United States in "counterinsurgency" techniques, have been a recurrent feature of the Latin American scene from the 1920s and 1930s through the 1960s into the present. Of the colonel's final ambition to "erase every vestige of a corrupt and scandalous regime supported by the foreign invader," Joset remarks that the colonel describes "exactly the political regime of more than one Latin American state in the twentieth century" (229; 320 and n. 44). The colonel's powerless rage only augments his powerlessness when a faceless enemy punishes that anger in a slaughter of innocents.

The death squads and murderous extirpations flourish after the colonel has retired from revolution and given up resistance. Their function is prophylactic, and they create a longing for the equivocal potency they prevent. The younger, more vigorous colonel had ties not only with a continuing revolution in Colombia (through Victor Medina) but also with the most successful revolution of the 1960s. At the height of his power the colonel wears a uniform like the one Fidel still wears: plain denim without insignia. When he shoots General Moncada, he uses a peculiarly modern jargon: "Remember, old friend . . . I'm not shooting you. It's the revolution that's shooting you" (153; 235). Moncada and Col. Aureliano Buendía's friendship is based on that between turn-of-the-century Colombian generals. Shooting one's friends and shifting responsibility to the revolution come from more radical periods. Assassinating Teófilo Vargas, burning the widow Moncada's house, and shooting Moncada with self-justifying efficiency form part of the novel's critique of revolution, revolutionaries, and power.

Far more sympathetic than the colonel at this period is the anagrammatic Gen. José Raquel Moncada (Macondo). On 26 July 1953, Fidel Castro and a small band made an unsuccessful attack on the Moncada barracks. From that attack, the Cuban revolutionary move-

A Political Reading

ment took its cognomen, the 26th of July Movement, and 26 July remains a Cuban national day of celebration. "Moncada" is a name associated with the origins of a revolutionary movement that later triumphs. Like "Victor Medina," it is the less familiar aspect of a famous event. But although Col. Aureliano Buendía shoots Moncada (takes the barracks, as Fidel did not), he loses the war (as Fidel did not).

Losing makes him a more sympathetic character once again, but its other costs are enormous. How does one weigh Moncada's life and the widow's house against the colonel's 17 sons? Add in the lives of the "brother of the forgotten Colonel Magnífico Visbal and his seven-year–old grandson" (224; 315: "forgotten" is right: no one has yet identified him). Also add in the lives of the striking banana workers. Moncada, his widow, Teófilo Vargas, and the young officer who suggested the shooting of Vargas stand out as individuals, but the scale sinks with the weight of the bodies on the other side.

In its ideological, intentional thrust, the text sympathizes with the colonel as an implementer of radical reforms, a restorer of land to rightful proprietors, a fighter for the rights of the dispossessed and unacknowledged. The colonel is also the only radical among the Buendías until his almost mad, equally defeated great-nephew, the labor organizer José Arcadio Segundo. The colonel's brother José Arcadio and his nephew Arcadio destroy the egalitarian community of the patriarch, while his great-nephew and namesake Aureliano Segundo colludes in the prosperity of the gringo banana company. Except for the colonel and José Arcadio Segundo, the Buendías are Snopeses.

Critics who charge that *One Hundred Years of Solitude* abandons the struggle for a free, revolutionary Latin America must think that without victory there is no struggle. In its radical critique of conventional politics, the novel argues both the futility and the necessity of resistance. Against the colonel's will to justice, the politicians in black coats weave their flimsy webs of political compromise, discussion, delay, and deferral that the colonel cannot break through. The politicians are all the same, whether they meet in cold early morning cafés

77

to munch on who said what or send specious letters of condolence to their enemies or file infinite briefs for the banana company. That radical critique comprehends a critique of radicalism. Whether it carries that radical critique to the explicit endorsement of a revolutionary position, the reader's judgment on "Rodrigo" may decide.

"Rodrigo" is not, of course (see Chapter 9), the only instance of a coincidence between the personal and the political. García Márquez follows the historically free account of Col. Aureliano Buendía's wars with the historically precise account of "the events in the banana zone of the Department of Magdalena between November 1928 and March 1929," including the "incident" at the Ciénaga train station in December 1928. In 1928 Álvaro (Cepeda Samudio), who shares with Aureliano Babilonia a complicity based on real facts that no one believed in, was a four-year-old living in a house overlooking the Ciénaga square. His account of the massacre, *La casa grande* (1962; The big house), preceded García Márquez's. When García Márquez also reconstructs the strike, he unites a personal myth and a political paradigm. A reality erased by tacit agreement and official historiography is reestablished, and the memory loss caused by insomnia plagues is undone.

At the personal level, he restores an event erased from his own high school history textbooks. Like the standard textbooks of other nations, Colombia's Henao and Arrubla drop unpleasant details in favor of abstract "disturbances of public order . . . martial law," followed properly, promptly by "reestablishment of public order."[8] Restoring the details, García Márquez overcomes the obsessive, frustrated powerlessness imprisoning those who possess a knowledge denied not only by power but also by one's friends at school, far from the banana zone.

At the public level, the episode of the banana massacre stands as a paradigm for all those sacrifices that the victors erase, from Dinajpur to Ciénaga to Tienamen Square. Writing cannot stop such events from occurring and recurring, but it can make them known. As Milan Kundera put it, "The struggle of man against power is the struggle of memory against forgetting."[9] The accuracy with which García Márquez recounts the events suggests a commitment to the historic reality of such events, a commitment better served by history than by denunciation. At the same time, he allows himself the hyperbole of "3,000 dead," as if in our moral accounts 3,000 matter more than 30.

García Márquez's account of the banana strike is, as Lucila Mena pointed out, a textbook case of Alejo Carpentier's *lo real maravilloso* (the "marvelous real").[10] There were two strikes, separated in reality by ten years, and by an undetermined lapse of time in the novel. The banana company was the same United Fruit Company in whose interests the United States destroyed Guatemalan democracy in 1954 when the government became too left-wing for its tastes. (That event is the subject of Miguel Angel Asturias's *Week-end en Guatemala* [1957]. Guatemala has not yet recovered the democratic institutions it possessed before U.S. intervention.) The banana boom created a sudden prosperity that brought on the "leafstorm" of García Márquez's fictions. (Its poetic equivalent is the miraculous proliferation of Petra Cotes's animals.) The company "changed the seasons and the course of the river" by constructing its own irrigation network; it paid workers in scrip redeemable at company stores for goods brought in by the banana fleets that would otherwise have had to return empty from New Orleans. It had its own train and telegraph lines and constituted a state within a state.

In 1918 workers struck, demanding wage increases, an end to scrip payments, and working conditions improved so as to conform to the conditions mandated by Colombian labor law. Support for the workers was widespread in the region, signaled in the fiction by the fact that "even" the priest approves and finds the workers' demands to be in accord with the law of God. The company agreed to consult with its Boston office, but nothing happened. Ten years later, there was another strike. The workers petitioned, raising the same and additional demands. Among their demands was that the company recognize that it had workers.

The demand was necessary because the banana-cropping system used contract labor. Workers worked on a piecework basis, in the hire of foremen-contractors. They moved from plantation to plantation, and because they were not directly employed by the banana growers, the growers were able to evade the provisions of Colombian labor law that mandated protections for workers such as latrines, hospitals, and accident insurance. The use of contract labor meant that United Fruit did not have workers of its own; it hired only the contractors. That fact lay behind the now famous and very real determination of a Colombian court that, indeed, the banana company had no workers.[11]

In describing the massacre of striking workers at the train station, García Márquez follows the account of the general, Carlos Cortés Vargas, who issued the decrees, ordered the firing, and oversaw the "mopping up" operation after the massacre. Labor organizers and sympathizers "disappeared" in a pattern that has become more familiar to us in recent years, from Argentina, El Salvador, Chile, and so on. The general and the novelist agree that the army was called in to break the strike, that saboteurs were interfering with the work of scabs, that a crowd assembled at the train station to await a mediator, that they were ordered by Decree No. 1 to disperse or the army would fire, that the army fired, that there was more violence in the days that followed as the army, under Decree No. 4, restored order and eliminated hooligans. Where the accounts differ is the number of dead: Cortés Vargas testifies to 29 men. García Márquez uses the largest number reported in North American newspaper accounts, 3,000. Cortés Vargas does not contrast the playful, friendly activities of his men by day with the murderous disappearances they caused by night. But he allows that it was three months before martial law could be lifted and order declared restored. The novelist eliminates the three months and has order declared at once.

The point, again, is that the narrative restores to reality an event that the "official story" denies. The story recovered here is rather minor by the standards of modern atrocities, just as the Terror of the French Revolution dwindles to nothing beside our gulags and holocausts. But the act of remembering is the paradigmatic act: it is the act of consciousness that creates a conscience in us.

9

Principles of Construction

One Hundred Years of Solitude is a technical tour de force that not only offers itself up to its reader for multiple readings but also forces multiple readings on the least willing reader. Having performed a few of the infinite number of readings possible, let us take a brief look at some of the structural features that prevent the reader from coming to rest. Briefly put, the novel seems elusive because it is both decentered and episodic. It is highly specific and detailed in its images, characters, and events; the narrator is more interested in telling us about his characters and their world than he is in telling us what anything or everything means.

The narrative tone in One Hundred Years of Solitude is often described as uniform or as identical with the characters' point of view. The reason for this not entirely accurate account is the narrator's imperturbability in the face of strange events. He expresses no surprise at the reappearance of the dead or astonishment that a room (Melquíades's) should be seen differently by different characters: luminous and untouched, or decayed and filthy. Nor does he ever judge his characters as primitive, ignorant, or defective in historical consciousness. But while the narrator is indeed serene and unflappable, his relation to the text is unstable. Sometimes he explains things to us from a perspective superior to his characters, as with José Arcadio Buendía's imagination that always went beyond miracles and magic. Sometimes he relates events from his characters' point of view, as when José Arcadio Buendía greets the aged ghost of Prudencio Aguilar. Sometimes he lets us see that the character greeting the ghost is deluded, as when we understand that José Arcadio Buendía takes Ursula for Prudencio Aguilar when she cares for him and talks to him.

Sometimes he deliberately confuses us, as when, without explanation, Arcadio replaces his uncle, Col. Aureliano Buendía, in a prediction of death by firing squad. Sometimes he deliberately deceives us, as in his account of the mysterious murder of José Arcadio. Sometimes he may be putting us on or he may be echoing an unidentified voice or he may be serious: it is impossible to be sure, as when he tells us that Melquíades really had been through death (55; 125). Sometimes he simply dislocates us by introducing an unfixed frame of reference, as when the little yellow train arrives "for the first time eight months late" (210; 299). Eight months late? Eight months late for whom? Relative to what? You ask in vain. Often—though it seems in recollection to be always—he constructs a double reading for us, creating anticipations of events before they occur, creating memories and nostalgia for events that still exist, in narrative time, in the reader's future.

Only once does anything make him angry, that "dragon," those "*hijos de la misma madre*" ("sons of the same mother," "bitch" in the English translation), the Antioquian army that obeyed the command to fire on the banana workers. Not only does he interpret for us as we read, but he also reinterprets the narrative we have read when it is read by Aureliano Babilonia as the manuscripts of Melquíades (and reread by us). There is more, but we might as well conclude with what the author condemns critics for overlooking. The narrator is animated, always, by an "immense compassion" for his "poor creatures,"[1] for the unloved Fernanda, the forgotten Santa Sofía de la Piedad, who cuts the throat of her own dead son, for the frightened homosexual José

Arcadio, and for the slimy green teeth, glowing in the dark, of José Arcadio Segundo. (Compassion does not preclude comedy.) The narrator is even busier than those ants, and since the novel is almost entirely narrated, with very little dialogue, the success of the novel belongs essentially to his quick changes within a serene, imperturbable tone that does not prefer one aspect of reality to another or depreciate any at the expense of others.

Readers can always locate a reality behind the narrator's mirages. To do so, they have to shift codes as rapidly as the narrator does. And, as soon as they have identified the metaphor literalized, the wish fulfilled, the text echoed, as soon as they have cut through the jungle to "reality," the text behind them closes up and resumes its mask. Is the reader required to cut through to reality, or can the text be read as just an imaginary world? Both. Much of the time, the reader cannot help seeing two realities simultaneously (the magnets, flying carpets, television). Relative to the characters, their loves, lives, and losses, the reader can read *One Hundred Years of Solitude* as any other novel is read. But from time to time, the narrator tosses in an episode that cannot immediately be understood, that stymies the reader completely. Such episodes force readers to try to cut through the impenetrable image. Since the image is impenetrable, readers will fail, but they also will not be content unless they try. The ice and the insomnia plague are such images. The ice is far more impenetrable than the insomnia plague, but the insomnia plague will stop the reader who got past the ice without difficulty the first time.

The teller has to have something to tell, of course, and what is told also multiplies the variety of the text. Instead of one story, it tells many stories; instead of one character with whom the reader identifies, or one generation of characters in whose relationships the reader is interested, the novel shifts from character to character, from generation to generation. It lacks the protagonist who always unifies an episodic structure in Western literature, and it lacks the unified action whose resolution is conventionally the ultimate (as it were) source of meaning in a text.

The characters themselves are fragmented by the episodic succession of the narrative. At first they seem to be types: the founder, the matriarch, the macho, the spinster, the *cachaco* (uppity highlander), the homosexual. However strange the events that happen around them or however hyperbolic such attributes as José Arcadio's penis, the characters represent central cultural types, not aberrant or deviant or weird marginal figures. (The exception is Remedios the Beauty. As an idiot or as the only rational being in the house, she deviates, and her fate is appropriately unlike any one else's.) When the scattered parts of these characters are assembled, however, they yield characters of substantial, novelistic complexity.

The reader putting together the fragments the narrative provides may end up "writing" a very different kind of novel out of the materials supplied by this one. What sort of woman could cut the throat of her own dead son, as Santa Sofía de la Piedad does? What weakness in José Arcadio Buendía's character leads him to allow a year to pass before he consummates his marriage? Col. Aureliano Buendía loves a prepubescent girl, loses himself in the solitude of power, and foresees the room of Melquíades filled with trash. The first leads toward a psychoanalytic reading of the character or the amorous habits of his family, the second connects him with history and the futility of historical action, the third with the question of reality and unreality. But all are the colonel, even if, laid out this way, it seems a bit difficult to fit them into one body. To take in the full complexity of the characters with all their dispersed characteristics is to construct characters and a novel of a different sort than García Márquez has written. But the one he has written provides many opportunities for the reader to write his or her own.

At first, the structure, if not the events, of the novel seems conventional enough. The novel seems to promise that it has both a plot and a protagonist in the history of Col. Aureliano Buendía and his wars. But no single character dominates the whole of the action, and no single action (or intertwined or parallel actions) extends the length of the narrative. Novels, it is unfair to say, always end with the death, marriage, or long meditative walk on the beach of a principal character.

At worst, there is a scene "many years later" with the heroine now plump and reproductive or "many years before" with our hero returning to his point of origin. Something occurs that resolves the character's fate and ties up the action, even if tying up the action only means a significant, suggestive, meaning-fraught pause to enable the author to stop. If nothing happens to change the character's life (as frequently happens these days), his or her consciousness is explored and transformed, and that makes all the difference.

What does not happen is what happens in *One Hundred Years of Solitude*. The opening sentence promises a principal character, Col. Aureliano Buendía, whose life and career should provide a conventional structure of novelistic expectation. But neither his life nor his career constitutes the whole of the action, and even during his wars, the actions of other characters are not subordinate to the colonel. Instead, such episodes as the loves of Rebeca and Amaranta, the madness of José Arcadio Buendía, and the discoveries of Ursula parallel the love and loss of Remedios Moscote by Aureliano. Then he and his wars are pushed from the center for the loves of Amaranta, Arcadio, and Aureliano José, the murder of José Arcadio, and the death of José Arcadio Buendía. By the end of Chapter 9, not halfway through the book, the wars end, and the colonel drifts into the obscurity of his workshop to die at the end of Chapter 13. The circus animals desert him on a street filled with flying ants. Without him, the book moves on through several more generations in seven more chapters to end with different characters in a different world.

Nor does any other character replace the colonel as protagonist or stay with us until the end, the last page of the novel. The women last longer, and the novel depends heavily on the reader's identification with them. Readers sometimes confess to a terrible sense of loss or an overwhelming nostalgia when Ursula dies. Even more stunning is the shock of Pilar Ternera's death at the beginning of the last chapter. Like Ursula when Rebeca is discovered, we had forgotten she was alive, and now she is dead. The last Buendías do not know their relation to her, so remote has she become from the continuing life of the family.

But the women's lives do not shape the action or provide narrative structure. The only other novel I know so careless of the conventions of Western novel plotting is Lady Murasaki's *The Tale of Genji*. Since Lady Murasaki wrote hers in eleventh-century Japan, she has an excuse. García Márquez does it on purpose. He uses the colonel as a structural prop for the first half of the fiction and then kicks the prop away. (Not easily: García Márquez describes the day he had to kill Col. Aureliano Buendía as a day he dreaded.)

It is a risky gesture. The reader loses the clue to the direction of the narrative line, the convention of identification with a single character is violated, and the reader's attention disperses among the many new characters in the family of Aureliano Segundo. What García Márquez accomplishes, however, is very important. He prevents the significance of his fiction from terminating or seeming to terminate in an individual, in a single character or a single action. If the novel ended with the death of Col. Aureliano Buendía, we could comfortably sum up by saying the novel was about the futility of political action, the pointlessness of war, the inability to love. The novel is, of course, about all those things, but it is also about more than those, and it is about more than one life. It shatters what seemed to be a center in order to bring the wider historical, cultural, metaphysical, and literary implications of the narrative to the surface. The novel lives in its particular details, characters, and events, but its purposes and interests extend to the whole world that it has evoked, a world that exists in time as well as in space, through generations as well as in a remembered place.

Although the de-centering of the novel has been represented here in terms of something missing, a lack, it is in part to the de-centering that the novel owes the popularity that still puzzles its author.[2] While the restless activities of the young fill the page and occupy the reader's attention, the reader rests securely, babe in arms, on the stability provided by the mothers, Ursula and Pilar. Meanwhile, the narrative brims with episodes, characters, and richly elaborated language so that there are no vacancies save that periodically opened by the word *solitude*. Although de-centered, the text is full (not unlike the world we live in). It creates multiple, momentary, successive centers, and in doing so gives wholeness and integrity to lives that would otherwise be subordinated to a protagonist. The presence of a protagonist or a single center means the exclusion, subordination, or marginalization of all other contenders. *One Hundred Years of Solitude* is more democratic, pluralist, and inclusive than that, and it makes its characters, for a moment, the heroes of their own lives. In turn, the combination of de-centering with fullness enables readers to find their own place (or their own mirror) within the text.

Once the usual narrative conventions have hooked us into the novel, García Márquez can discard them because of the novel's extraordinary surface complexity. At first, the novel does not seem complex at all, especially if complexity is taken to mean difficulty. As Ricardo Gullón put it, García Márquez seems to have rediscovered "the lost art of story-telling."[3] The endless stream of incidents, punctuated by bizarre moments and peopled by dramatic characters, moves with a rapidity that puts airport fiction to shame. Promising violence and discovery, the opening reintroduces us to the world of fairy-tale quests and childhood astonishment. Once out of the "latency" period of boyish explorations and discoveries, the novel discovers sex.

As Fausto Avendaño pointed out in his analysis, "*El factor del best-seller en* Cien años de soledad,"[4] and Gustavo Alvarez Gardeazábal confirmed in "*Las formas de hacer el amor en* Cien años de soledad," the vigorous sexuality of the *macondanos* teases the reader on as the novel penetrates the private life of the bedroom (bathroom, hammock, violet fields). The text presents no impediments, save one, to an easy, rapid, and superficial reading. The single impediment is the confusion deliberately provoked by the recurrent names José, Arcadio, Aureliano, and their combinations.[5] (The women's names present no difficulty, though at least one critic did manage to confuse Remedios the Beauty with her great-aunt Remedios Moscote.) That confusion is the reader's first hint of the underlying complexity in the patterning of the text.

Once we notice the presence of repetition and contrast, patterns begin to multiply. Everywhere we look, we see parallels, echoes, contrasts, emblems of the whole. Nothing happens only once in *One Hundred Years of Solitude*, and nothing happens the same way twice. This narrative that has seemed so lucid, so transparent, so easy, begins to overload with signification. Such patterning prevents the narrative from becoming tediously episodic, as almost happens to a few of Cervantes's *Exemplary Tales*. With so many patterns, no single pattern can hold *the* meaning of the text. Instead, the perception and ordering of patterns figure among the meanings of the text.

There are two principal kinds of pattern, the warp and the woof of the narrative web: diachronic transformations and synchronic repetitions.[6] Lucila Mena has described both very well. The diachronic dimension of the narrative is dynamic, characterized by change, development, chronological time, and historical becoming. It constitutes a horizontal axis running the length of the narrative. The synchronic dimension is static, mythic, characterized by eternal models, universal archetypes, stopped time.[7] It constitutes a vertical axis of repetitions without external causes. Multiple patterning occurs along both the synchronic and the diachronic dimensions of the narrative.

Along the diachronic dimension stretch both literary and historical patterns. Western literature's originating texts, the Hebrew Bible and the Hellenic tragedy, provide the basic structures. From Genesis to Apocalypse (or Revelation, a book), the narrative repeats the Bible. Over the same period, it ostentatiously defers the incest of *Oedipus Tyrannos*. Within those literary limits, historical narratives unfold. Carried by the novel's highly specific details are a history of science and technology, a history of economic development and decline, a social history of Latin America, a political history of Colombia, and a regional history of the banana zone. There is also a history of changing female roles as the characters in the female line mark an erratic progress from sexual inhibition and economic productivity (Ursula) to sexual liberation and economic uselessness (Amaranta Ursula, Meme).

Also marking time's changes is a literary history of the West: folktale is followed by epic and romance, the bourgeois novel, and the self-reflexive fictions of modernity. Literary genres shift with characters and episodes: José Arcadio Buendía's quest for gold follows folktale patterns. The founding of Macondo falls under epic, as do the wars of José Arcadio Buendía's son, the colonel. The period of Amaranta and Rebcca's love for Pietro Crespi and Aureliano's for Remedios Moscote is evidently romantic, as the house fills with love and poetry; while the family-centered, adulterous, and mysteriously rich Aureliano Segundo and his radical labor organizer twin bring us to the bourgeois, economic novel. We end with the self-reflexive fiction and the self-absorbed adolescent of the modern novel. These literary types also correspond to stages of historical, social, and economic development: founding, civil wars, social and economic progress or growth, and marginalized modernity. (We have inventive explorer José Arcadio Buendía; the warrior or *caudillo* Col. Aureliano Buendía and his brother José Arcadio, the *latifundista*; the bourgeois and radical great-grandsons, Aureliano Segundo the prosperous and José Arcadio Segundo the labor organizer; and finally, the bookish, adolescent, intellectual great-great-great-grandson Aureliano Babilonia. Aureliano's friends are also observers, readers, and writers: Álvaro on his endless train ride, Gabriel in Paris sleeping by day and writing by night, the Catalan with his spidery manuscripts.) Dry as these bones are, the patterns perform a skeleton's service. They enable readers to be entirely absorbed by the sharp, luminous, comical details of an active panorama, yet to recognize where they are in an otherwise unfamiliar landscape.

While more than one historical narrative is at work in the fiction, the tendency of each has often been described as a movement from myth, the timelessness of epic and origins, into historical time. The novel actually begins with a sentence that straddles both time frames. Before the firing squad, Col. Aureliano Buendía is "in history," after Melquíades's second death in Macondo and before his final disappearance. Threatened by history, the colonel remembers a moment from his childhood (life's prehistoric period) in a mythic setting, before Melquíades's first death. When Melquíades returns from his first death (on the sands of Singapore) to halt the insomnia plague and to die a second time in the waters of Macondo, historic time begins. History means written documents, and at that period Melquíades begins to write his mysterious parchments. At the end of the novel, Macondo passes out of historical time into fictive time, the time of the book.

If the novel has a fundamental ploy, it is to enhance the experience of recognition by estranging the reader from the text. Certainly the management of time works that way. The narrator often puzzles his reader by remembering events before they happen. Later the reader understands what he was referring to, as in Amaranta's weaving of her shroud. Or present events are treated from the perspective of their future repercussions, as in the nostalgia evoked by the little yellow train the moment it arrives. Or two present moments are juxtaposed, as when José Arcadio Buendía finds the galleon covered with orchids, and many years later his son finds it burned out in a field of poppies. Or a past that belongs to the reader and the novel, not to the character, is heaped up, as when Aureliano Babilonia sinks into the chair in which Rebeca embroidered, Amaranta played Chinese checkers with Gerineldo Márquez, and Amaranta Ursula sewed baby clothes. To Aureliano's nostalgia for Amaranta Ursula, the text adds the reader's (and the narrator's) for all the others. Such management of time makes even the first reading of the novel seem to be a second reading. The narrator's habit of predicting things means that when readers first happen on an episode, they already know it. They are already remembering it, rather than encountering it unmediated for the first time. In Michael Palencia-Roth's formulation, the line (diachronic, chronological) turns into a circle. As the narrative carries the reader forward, other, synchronic patterns swirl across the surface.

The best account of the synchronic patterning of *One Hundred Years of Solitude* is Josefina Ludmer's, supplemented by Lydia Hazera for the female characters.[8] Ludmer summed up the novel's patterning this way: "Similitude and alteration, reflections and doubles, same and other, paradox, irony, symmetry, complementarity: a continuous work of variations, multiplications, fusions, inversions, substitutions, metamorphosis and anamorphosis operate in personages, names, scenes, objects, actors, paragraphs in *One Hundred Years of Solitude*: we're dealing with an essentially baroque space, saturated with a kind of cosmic narcissism" (145). She did leave out "phrases," which are subjected to the same kind of treatment as persons and everything else, but otherwise she covered the ground. We will not try to duplicate that effort of insight and ingenuity, but we should mark a few of the ways in which such patterns work.

Patterns first press themselves into awareness through the repetition and variation of men's names. The reader's first impression of the novel is that all the men are named either José Arcadio or Aureliano and that it is impossible to tell one from another. In fact, while the names are all repeated, each character has a distinctive variant until the end of the novel (José Arcadio Buendía, José Arcadio, Aureliano, Arcadio, Aureliano José, José Arcadio Segundo, and Aureliano Segundo). Then Aureliano Babilonia is called just Aureliano, as the colonel was at the beginning, and José Arcadio, his homosexual uncle, is called just José Arcadio, like the macho José Arcadio, the colonel's brother. From one parallel, others grow. The inversion homosexual/macho forms an ironic identity/contrast. Both the homosexual and the macho return to Macondo after long travels, both find an unconventional love in Macondo, and both are murdered by those they have abused over money. Such patterns begin to emerge as soon as one puts any character beside another, but with repetition, there is always variation, not identity.

Having established the principle that confusing repetitions occur within the simple onward flux, the narrative then nudgingly suggests that the reader really ought to begin to interpret this continual change, to make patterns and impose order on this apparent chaos of similarities with differences. About halfway through the novel, at the beginning of Chapter 10, Ursula develops a hypothesis: the contrast between lucid and withdrawn Aurelianos and active, enterprising, tragic José Arcadios, with a mix-up in the twins José Arcadio Segundo and Aureliano Segundo. The narrator adds his hint to Ursula's, for the sentence that opens the tenth chapter conspicuously echoes the opening sentence of the novel. ("Years later on his deathbed Aureliano Segundo would remember the rainy afternoon in June when he went into the bedroom to meet his first son" [174; 258]; "Many years later, before the firing squad, Colonel Aureliano Buendía would remember that distant afternoon when his father took him to discover ice" [11; 71]. The parallels are more exact in Spanish, where the verbs "discover" and "meet" are both "*conocer*.") With that license to categorize provided by the narrative itself, a mad categorizer is unleashed in many readers. The reader should be warned: there is a great danger that he or she will begin to seek out *unduplicated* episodes, as well as predictions that are forgotten and that neither come true nor fail to come true. At that moment, the reader may find in the mirror the glassy stare of José Arcadio Segundo in Melquíades's room, or the whole novel may begin to swirl like the manuscripts of Melquíades, "when" and "then" vanishing.

Things start simply enough, with obvious contrasts between the first pair of brothers, José Arcadio and Aureliano: the easy sexuality of the first, the difficulties of the other. Both succeed with Pilar, but José Arcadio succeeds with his young gypsy girl, and Aureliano fails with the equally young prostitute. The dominant organ for José Arcadio is his preternatural penis, for Aureliano his eyes—the obvious contrasts between them generalize to include body and head, sexuality and clairvoyance. The sexual contrasts are repeated at the political-economic level: José Arcadio seizes land by violence and the threat of violence, and both Liberal and Conservative governments acquiesce. The radical Col. Aureliano Buendía restores land to its rightful owners, and both Liberals and Conservatives oppose him. Thanatos herself recognizes their differences, their strengths and their weaknesses: invulnerable to attempted murders, Aureliano is unable to kill himself when he tries and dies old, while urinating outdoors. José Arcadio dies young, murdered, indoors, with blood streaming from his head at the ear. José Arcadio's blood seeks his mother; Col. Aureliano Buendía once pissed on his father's ghost at the same tree. José Arcadio's corpse reeks of powder (perhaps suggesting that the deliberately misleading story of his death stinks, even from underground); Col. Aureliano Buendía's body is found only when Santa Sofía de la Piedad notices the vultures descending as she is throwing out the garbage.

Now that is all fairly obvious, surely, and we can continue the activity of parallel, antithesis, chiasmus and zeugma through Aureliano José and Arcadio, Fernanda and Ursula, Pilar Ternera and Petra Cotes, and so on. More can be done with some parallels than others, but they extend to what seem to be the minutest details, and new examples turn up at every reading. We all know on our first reading (it is the narrator's first trick) that Col. Aureliano Buendía is not shot in front of the firing squad and that Arcadio is. But it was long before I observed that Remedios Moscote, the colonel's child-wife, dies of a ruptured uterus with twins twisted inside her, while Santa Sofía de la Piedad, Arcadio's unmarried widow, gives birth to (Remedios's) twins after Arcadio, remembering Remedios in his last moment, is shot. Schematically put: young wife dead/husband before firing squad, not shot/husband lives to be old/twins die// wife lives to be old/husband before firing squad, shot/husband dies young/twins live. And the impatient gentle reader says, so what? I like to read novels, not parse them.

Impatience with other people's lists of parallels is entirely justified. It's a bit like diagramming sentences: it's fun to do yourself, but tedious to watch other people doing, unless they solve a problem for you in your own diagramming, or unless you catch them in a mistake. (That is to say, like other games, it is boring unless you are playing it, too.) What doing a little parsing shows, however, is the difference between the experience of reading the text and the actual structural underpinnings of the text.

The underlying structure of details is enormously complicated. To chart them all would require a text longer than *One Hundred Years of Solitude,* and the chart would have the same interest as those infinite chains generated in transformational grammars. Even though the reader may not care to embark on the enterprise of making such a chart, the presence of such an underlying structure of details makes a difference to the reading. Every time the reader makes a connection between one detail and another, he or she experiences a small, pleasant explosion of enlightenment. The same thing happens when the reader connects details in the novel to events outside the novel, of whatever category (biographical, technological, political, psychological, and so on). The experience of such recognitions is like having one's own private, mental fireworks display.

There are trade-offs, of course. This constant sensory teasing or gratification at the surface of the narrative forestalls the explosive intensity of a Sophocles or a Milton.[9] For García Márquez to achieve a comparable effect, he has to wrench his text off its ostensible ground in Macondo and catapult it into "a text."

At the stylistic level, the patterning is essential to the reader's sense of the text's density and richness, just as rhetorical and metaphorical manipulation of language is responsible for the richness and density of a Renaissance sonnet. The text fills with echoes. Within it we see a pattern of words striking in itself, whether or not we can assign any particular, extrinsic meaning to that pattern. The irrationality of the figure, its resistance to rational interpretation, is often part of its power. (Shifting patterns of metaphor in Shakespeare, of rhetorical figures in Sidney, and of rhymes in Pope work the same way.) An example of a powerful, irrational parallel is the carnival massacre and the striking workers' massacre. To recognize the parallel is chilling; to account for it, save as rhetorical contrast, impossible (I think). Ludmer's analogy with the baroque is very apt: there are no bare spots. Everywhere, moving figures and shifting spaces fill the eye.

When the figure does not resist rational interpretation but offers itself up as an increment to sense, then meaningful patterns begin to form. Once rational interpretation begins, meanings proliferate crazily along all the available codes. Is our concern or subject the novel as a whole? The presence of antitheses, of contradictory characters, episodes, and ideas, is essential to the impression of totality that the novel conveys. Is our concern the realistic basis for a serious story about a family and a town? The persistence of unconscious physical and psychological characteristics communicates family resemblance. Is our concern the relation between time, character, and memory? Repetitions mark the difference between an experience as it is lived and an experience as it is remembered. For Col. Aureliano Buendía in front of the firing squad, the memory of the ice is much thinner than the discovery of ice experienced and recorded in the first chapter. Has life thinned his memory so much, or does he retain, unarticulated, some of the ambivalent, disillusioning glory of that moment? For Aureliano Segundo, the "lived" narrative passes over almost without notice the actual experience of seeing his first son, but as a memory on his deathbed the narrative marks it indelibly. So, too, for the departure of his daughter Amaranta Ursula; but did he remember anything of Meme, his other daughter? Only by enumerating the parallels can we observe what has been left out, and omissions, we all know, emit infinite implications.

Such parallels explain, in part, what it means to call Macondo the "city of mirrors." As Suzanne Jill Levine has reminded us, the novel is "a speaking mirror." It reflects a world, and within that world every event mirrors another. Yet every reflection differs from its original, and no event occurs the same way twice. Looking for the face of the real Macondo, we see an image distorted, repeated, and so endlessly duplicated, that it mocks us with a carnival of masks. Macondo is the city of mirrors because the book of Macondo is a mirrored room (and vice versa).

The city of mirrors (or mirages) is also a city that lures readers and characters on, past the mirage of the colonel before the firing squad, past Fernanda's "accepting the miracle" (rejected by outsiders) of Remedios's ascension, past Aureliano Segundo's Divine Providence Raffles, to the final dissipation of illusion in the novel's last lines. In the desert, wanderers with thirsty eyes find only lines of heat, not the alluring oasis. So Macondo's reader finds not a new world, but mere words on parchment—not "the meaning of it all," but the end of a manuscript and the other reality of language. For a brief, illusory instant, Macondo was also a city of ice. A fundamental, irreducible, mysterious, and multi-interpretable reality, the great block of ice opens the novel and closes its first chapter. José Arcadio Buendía's fertile imagination turns it into the hallucinatory image of a city of ice, another mirage created by desire. In the light of common day and the hands of his grandchildren, the city of ice melts into a less romantic but more useful ice factory.[10] García Márquez's ironic, affectionate art creates and dissolves the illusion. The speaking mirror having spoken, he breaks it.

10

Magic Realism: Does He or Doesn't He?

> It is the discovery of a whole new world. One paints pots and
> piles of rubbish and sees these things in a completely different
> way as if one had never before seen a pot. One paints a land-
> scape, trees, houses, vehicles, and one sees the world anew.
> One discovers like a child a land of adventure.
>
> —Grethe Jurgens[1]

So perfect is the balance between the strange and the familiar in *One
Hundred Years of Solitude* that readers often emphasize one at the
expense of the other, as with the glass that is either half-full or half-
empty. For Anglo-American readers one great delight of the fiction is
the constant renewal of a sense of surprise, as if the imagination were
being reborn. For many Spanish-American readers, the novel's essential
virtue is that it renders, with "beauty and humor" (Fuentes's phrase),
a world and people they know. Anglo-American critics always provide
their lists of impossible happenings, levitating priests and sailing virgins, while Spanish-American critics often insist that there is nothing
"magical" in the novel, that Spanish-American reality is like that.
García Márquez himself falls in the second camp. Every event, he
insists, has a basis in reality, and he is always eager to cite examples
that show reality imitating his fiction. Both are right, of course, or both
are wrong. If this world were not distinctly bizarre, it would not be
necessary for Spanish-American critics to insist, again and again, that
it is realistic. If this world were as purely bizarre or fantastic as Anglo-

American critics often make it seem, no one would marvel at the wonders it contains or make long, delighted lists of marvels. Noticing the wonders is a silent acknowledgment that the text reposes—or spins—on the stability of truth.

"Magic realism" is the term often used to describe the characteristic mingling of the real and the fantastic in *One Hundred Years of Solitude,* and the reader will, naturally enough, want to know what the term means and how to use it. That would be a simple need to meet were it not for considerable disagreement within the critical community as to what the term means and how it should be used. In 1973 the International Association of Iberoamericanists devoted its proceedings to the question, and the disputants produced so many different and incompatible definitions that it was proposed the term be abandoned forever.[2] Even that proposal failed to win assent. The quarreling persists because some critics find indispensable a term that others find mortally offensive. Over this phrase, unknown to the combatants, a guerrilla war is being fought against Anglo-American cultural imperialism; the cause is just, but, in the Anglo-American context, doomed. Losing the Battle of the Phrase north of the border, anti-magic realists have the consolation that they win the War of Understanding the Text. Equally hopeless is the situation of those snipers, as isolated as Japanese stragglers on a Pacific island, who want to hold magic realism to its original sense, undistorted by the impact of García Márquez.

In current Anglo-American usage, magic realism is a narrative technique that blurs the distinction between fantasy and reality. Angel Flores first applied the term "magical realism" to twentieth-century Spanish-American writing in 1955, using Kafka and de Chirico as the European models and Borges as the great American exemplar. Unlike other postenlightenment forms of the fantastic, magical realism treated fantastic events as entirely natural, or real. "Magic" meant almost any deviation from the conventions of nineteenth-century European realism, as long as the style was precise and lean, the effect surprising, and the plotting "logically conceived: well-rounded or projected

Sketch of García Márquez by Lowell Boyers, 1982.

against an infinite perspective."[3] Flores's account omitted the folkloric (Indian, African, or mestizo) that others now often regard as an essential characteristic or source of Latin American magic realism.

When the folkloric is taken as essential to magic realism, Miguel Angel Asturias and Alejo Carpentier replace Borges as exemplars, and Borges is shifted off toward "fantastic literature."[4] "Magic" ceases to be the fantastic and becomes the real practice and belief of the folk, related from their perspective. When this definition is strictly adhered to, *One Hundred Years of Solitude* ceases to be a magic realist text, since many of its events are inescapably fantastic: insomnia plagues just do not happen anywhere. As a result, some critics prefer to call García Márquez's practice "fantastic realism," reserving "magic" for those who still practice it.[5]

Still others prefer to keep the term "magic realism" closer to its origins in art criticism. In 1925 the German art critic Franz Roh used the term to distinguish a new trend in modern painting that departed from expressionism's "fantastic, supraterrestrial, remote subjects" and "shocking exoticism."[6] That movement sought to represent "the strange, the eerie, the uncanny, the dreamlike," the magical in commonplace, everyday reality, or it infused the quotidian with a primitive or childlike naïveté. Through hard edges and sharp detail, artists rendered scenes of everyday life with a "precise realism enveloped in an atmosphere of lucid amazement."[7] In this usage "magic" is an effect or an aspect of technique rather than the feature of content that it is in other definitions. In *One Hundred Years of Solitude* this magic realism appears in the narrative voice, as well as in episodes such as the discovery of ice, when an ordinary object is made to seem "magical."

The beleaguered "strict constructionists" are not placated, however. They rule *One Hundred Years of Solitude* out of the magic realist canon because it contains fantastic episodes. John W. Ferguson, for example, following Enrique Anderson-Imbert, disqualified the novel as magic realism because of events such as the ascension of Remedios the Beauty, the insomnia plague, Melquíades's return from the dead, the map of the dead read by ghosts and followed by them, and so on.

Magic Realism

In this impeccable use, the term "magic realism" applies to García Márquez's writing after *The Autumn of the Patriarch*, but not to *One Hundred Years of Solitude, Autumn of the Patriarch*, or *Innocent Eréndira*. The later writings abandon the fantastic and, with it, the mythic ambitions of the master narratives in favor of imaginative elaborations that cling more closely to (modern urban notions of) the possible.

For the reader who has followed the twisting lines of these battles over nomenclature, there is a small reward in the recognition that García Márquez's practice in *One Hundred Years of Solitude* fuses elements of every definition and corresponds in its entirety to none. Linked with Borgesian or Kafkaesque magic realism through fantastic invention, *One Hundred Years of Solitude* also possesses a significant folkloric element in its representation of village culture.[9] It then fuses those two "magic realisms" in a lucid style affined to the third, as does García Márquez's account of the novel's project.

The principal challenge in writing *One Hundred Years of Solitude*, García Márquez explained after he had done it, was finding a style that would permit him to erase the barrier between fantasy and reality: "My most important problem was to destroy the line of demarcation that separates what seems real from what seems fantastic. Because in the world that I was trying to evoke, that barrier didn't exist."[10] The "problem" is technical or stylistic, as for Roh et al. Erasing the line between the real and the fantastic corresponds to Flores's "magical realism." The world "I was trying to evoke" is the real world of a real village, where the line to be erased has never existed.

So around we come again to the broad, current definition in which magic (all senses) and realism are equally features both of style and of content: magic realism is a technique that blurs the distinction between fantasy and reality. So confident is Anglo-American usage that, from London, Edwin Williamson has assured us there can be no dispute about this definition.[11] Not only has there already been considerable dispute, however, but passionate quarrels also continue over the unreality that attaches to "magic" in modern usage.

In much Anglo-American critical practice that relies on a definition derived from *One Hundred Years of Solitude,* such as Williamson's, "magic" or the fantastic is deemed to be content, while realism is relegated to background technique, illuminated by an occasional flash of "magical" style. The reality of the "world I was trying to evoke" is erased, to the great resentment of some readers. Inverting the earlier, also principally Spanish-American, objection that in *One Hundred Years of Solitude* García Márquez has replaced reality with fantasy, those readers care little for the subtleties of nomenclature or the history of taxonomy. But they care greatly for something perhaps more important, the political and intellectual consequences of our choices of words.

Anti-magic realists object to the way "magic" undermines the realism of "magic realism." The more the term is depended on as description, especially by readers unfamiliar with Latin America, the more "magic" displaces "reality." Irate Latin American critics quartered in Anglo-American universities object that their reality is forced to conform to Anglo-American norms. Julio Ortega has dismissed "the traditional notion of 'magic realism' [as] a conceptually poor representation of the *specific differences* that shape Latin American text and culture" (emphasis added).[12] Fernando Alegría has snapped rather sharply that Flores could not resist waving "the magic wand" to describe such disparate works as Asturias's *Legends of Guatemala* and *Men of Corn* or Carpentier's *The Lost Steps* and *The Kingdom of This World,* "books that abruptly dismantled the stage of regionalism which had been the one ring-circus of Latin American narrative for several generations." If the reality of *One Hundred Years of Solitude* seems strange to Europeans, that is only because they do not know its world.[13] Gregory Rabassa, a recruit from the Anglos, has delicately suggested that to speak of "magic realism" is to adopt "flat-headed nineteenth-century norms" of reality and magic.[14] In effect, Latin American reality is colonized by the term. A reality that one knows to be real is dismissed as fantastic or "magical," and that can be very annoying. If they lose the battle, however, the anti-magic realists win the war. The inhabitant of an isolated Mexican mountain town can say (as at least one has said) of the world of *One Hundred Years of*

Solitude, yes, that's what life is like here. "In the world that I was trying to evoke, that barrier didn't exist." The world García Márquez was trying to evoke is a world without the barrier that the term "magic realism" reimposes.

Anglo-American readers do not share that reality and cannot recognize it. So magic encroaches on the real, to the great increase of credulity. To take an unlikely example: We cannot fathom a world where a gypsy might say, when he next returns to town, that he died on the sands of Singapore, but didn't like being dead. It was too lonely. Paradoxically, we give such a statement more credence than it deserves or would get in its own context. We confuse what can be said to have happened with what has actually happened. Yes, Melquíades, you died on the sands of Singapore. Right—you say it, the children will believe it, so will some adults, why should we quarrel with a story that we would much rather repeat? And life goes on. There exist worlds in which such assertions will be made, and they will be received with different degrees of assent by different auditors (and readers). But it probably takes an Anglo-American critic to insist with entire seriousness that people really do come back from the dead in *One Hundred Years of Solitude.* That critic enjoys the excitement of a wish-fulfilling fantasy but never possesses the supple response that recognizes such an event as not "magic" but "real." Meant to evoke a continuum, magic realism often reerects a barren dichotomy.

In spite of the damage the term "magic realism" causes and the imperialism it promotes, it seems impossible (for an Anglo-American critic) to do without it. As Seymour Menton's taxonomy shows, many different relations between the real and the magical or the fantastic are comprehended under the term in García Márquez's practice, and it is essential to the effect of *One Hundred Years of Solitude.*[15] The principal competitive term is Alejo Carpentier's "marvelous [American] real" (*"lo real maravilloso americano"*).

Alejo Carpentier coined *"lo real maravilloso americano"* in the preface to *The Kingdom of This World* (1949). Like Roh's original magic realism, it was invented in opposition to surrealism and the fantastic. As González Echevarría has explained, Carpentier adopted the surrealist term "the marvelous" but dismissed the European surrealists' straining after marvelous effects. America's "hyperreality" had only to be represented as it is, and it would astonish Europeans as it had since Columbus.[16] The banana strike, the weather, the flora and fauna, bloody lilies and golden salamanders—in *One Hundred Years of Solitude* geographical and naturalist description and most political events are Carpentier's "marvelous reality." The marvelous appearance depends entirely on rendering: Rebeca's eating dirt, the child with a pig's tail, a plague of butterflies, a rain of dead birds, the seemingly interminable rains, the news-songs of Francisco the Man, the loss of 32 civil wars in 20 years, a strike in which the courts decree that the workers do not exist. These things happen. Entailing no violations of the laws of physics, they may be marvels, but they are not magic.

Since magical practices and folkloric beliefs, as well as the ironic incredulity of European consciousness, form part of American reality, they too may be comprehended by the marvelous real. Such boundary-blurring events, enacting folkloric beliefs that are real for some people though not for us, include the assumption of the virgin, Remedios the Beauty, the levitating priest, or the persistence of the dead. If such episodes are "marvelous" to the European eye, they may be "real" to the folk, who know more about them. But even if Melquíades now returns from the dead with more plausibility, the insomnia plague and the flying carpets still present difficulties.

Whether or not the reader chooses to apply the term "magic realism" to García Márquez has implications for how he or she understands the work. Menton is an exception, but one of the more distressing aspects of the use of the term is that it often produces in critics the fuzzy blur that Alegría, Ortega, and Rabassa so object to. As Alegría has indicated, magic realism has had a tendency to spread itself uniformly over a wide area, rather like an oil slick. It blankets different aspects of the text—the stylistic heightening and defamiliarization of the purists or the realistic rendering and fantastic content of popular use—and does not distinguish among them. Rather like "romanticism" or "classicism," the term takes on a life—or death—of its own. The critic begins to quarrel with a definition of his own devising, while the text sinks, cased in the concrete block of a critical term, to the reefs below. The specificity of the text's imagery, its rootedness in reality, the interplay between the real and the imagined are all lost in a uniform swirl of improbabilities.[17]

The loss of specificity and difference is troubling. To repeat Williamson's observation, García Márquez's technique in *One Hundred Years of Solitude* works precisely because it forces us to become conscious of differences. Without the specificity of difference, reading ends up with everything being the same as everything else, as in Richard Watson's brilliant parody (I trust) of a reading, "A Pig's Tail." Reading a "novel in English written by Gregory Rabassa based on a novel in Spanish by Gabriel García Márquez," Watson proved that life and death are the same, that one endeavor is like another, everything repeats everything else, you succeed, you fail, life goes on, death is inevitable, so it doesn't matter if you're alive or dead. It is a very persuasive reading (especially the bit about its not mattering if you're alive or dead), and it demonstrates, terrifyingly, what happens when similitude is substituted for difference in the novel. (Do read "A Pig's Tail"; it does a marvelous bit with Col. Aureliano Buendía's death and his "critical tool," and it is very funny.[18]) For Watson, the text has no reference to a real reality at all.

Watson and the Mexican who lives *One Hundred Years of Solitude* occupy different realities and read different books, Watson's more literary and clever, the Mexican's more real and richer. One denies the reality, the other the "magic," and both disdain debates over critical terms. But how then is the critic to describe that peculiar mix of the real and the fantastic that defines, if not magic realism, then the technique of *One Hundred Years of Solitude*? No one wants to call the novel an example of the fantastic. It is too firmly based in the powerful reality of the characters, their lives, and their politics. The author insists that he does not invent but elaborates reality, and the horror of many of his inventions confirms that fundamental, if sardonic, commitment to the real.

Replacing "magic realism" with the "marvelous real" has not

worked because readers know full well that it is not all real, however marvelous it is. People who have ashes put on their foreheads at Ash Wednesday mass may be "marked for life," but the ashes do wash off. Given that current usage blurs a once useful term, it would doubtless be best to abandon it for a term more specific to García Márquez, on the model of "Joycean," "Kafkaesque," or "Borgesian." Thomas Pynchon has put in for "Garciamarquesian," but other people's editors might find "*Garciamarquesianismo*" awkward.[19] For the duration, then, Anglo-American readers are likely to be stuck with the term. The only consolation is that in modern usage, the text itself has shaped the definition.

11

And If He Does, What Does It Mean?

Modern Myths and a Metaphysical Reading

Whatever one calls the distinctive mingling of realities that García Márquez practices in *One Hundred Years of Solitude,* its most obvious effect is to renovate a tired, old history of violence, exploitation, futility, and decay. When García Márquez defended himself against activist critics who had attacked the novel as escapist, he argued that Latin American readers had a right to see their reality transformed by literature. They did not need to read yet again of the poverty, dryness, and despair that they knew too well from living it.

As Williamson and others have observed, "magic realism" is a device of both alienation and attraction, and it enables that peculiar tone of great satire that gives *One Hundred Years of Solitude* much of its resilient toughness, a combination of irony, invention, and sympathy. That tone or manner is not one that readers of novels are much accustomed to. To those critics who believe the novel condemns Latin America to "a hopeless condition of historical failure, allowing no scope for change or free human action,"[1] it is difficult to resist recommending a course in *The Dunciad.*

If they take that course, the incorrigible ones will begin by asking,

Did Pope really mean that a giant yawn was overtaking the arts and civilization of Georgian England? That a goddess named Dulness was worshiped by all the world? That booksellers engaged in mud-diving contests to see who could rise with the darkest, deepest mud encrusting his brows? Did Pope really condemn Britain to the reign of "universal darkness," as his last line says ("Thy hand, Great Anarch, lets the curtain fall, / And universal darkness buries all")? Did he really condemn enlightenment Europe to "a hopeless condition of historical failure, allowing no scope for change or free human action"? Well, maybe, but probably not entirely. (Watson would tell us, yeah, everybody's as dumb as everybody else.) *The Dunciad* was written by no dunce, and it was dedicated to an unduncical admirer of Rabelais, Jonathan Swift. García Márquez has no first-person poet, but he makes much more explicit than Pope the fact that this "despairing" text is written. Whoever writes, however satirically or ironically, has not given up all hope.

I doubt that García Márquez has ever read Alexander Pope or ever will. But animating both writers is a deep skepticism about the direction of history in their time, a profound disengagement from the commercial, consumer culture that enriched them both, and a passion for literature and literary invention. Both were caught in the struggle between progress, a restless, onward, forward movement, and nostalgia, a longing for stasis, the unchanging, the past. For both, fantastic but "meaning-full" invention was the way to render an absurd, but compelling reality that had to be resisted. The political difference is that Pope's yawn put the future to sleep, while García Márquez has closed the books on the past.

To call magic realism a form of irony may seem perverse, but it explains the persistent frustration critics feel at the way the text slips away from them.[2] Irony derives from the *eiron,* the dissembler, the triumphant character in Greek comedy who subdues the braggart by his understatement, his "idiot face," and his persistence in saying something other than precisely what he means. The elusiveness of *One Hundred Years of Solitude* is characteristic of ironic texts that provide the reader with no explicit, fixed, authorially endorsed point of reference. Instead of providing a point of view with which to identify or to use as a measure, the text persistently undercuts its fixed points. It shows a world in which much is wrong or bizarre or perverse, but it does not sketch the alternatives to that world.

The expectation that a novel should promulgate some specific, positive moral system is very powerful, and modern readers tend to be uncomfortable if they cannot state a moral in positive terms. We still want our novels to provide us with myths to live by, but ironists do that only by the implications of their own practice. As a result, the critical, myth-seeking tendency to find *the* value that holds the novel together—love, solidarity, community, historical consciousness—is doomed. There simply is no such value to be found in the text. When García Márquez has been forced outside the novel, in interviews, to provide such a myth, he calls on two twentieth-century favorites, love and solidarity, and an eighteenth-century standby, happiness. In effect, he provides an inside-out reading of his novel to placate those readers uncomfortable with the novel's lack of a positive promise or premise.

To eliminate some of the contenders for moral purpose: solidarity and community are conspicuous by their absence. The era of their reign belongs to a mythic, prehistoric past so brief in duration that it is represented by a single sentence. Historical consciousness is useless without power: José Arcadio Buendía, Col. Aureliano Buendía, José Arcadio Segundo, Aureliano Babilonia, Gabriel Márquez, and Melquíades all possess knowledge that they are unable to use to any effect in the world. Nor is it clear what difference it would make in this world if they had power or different, more effective knowledge. Progress and prosperity, which are eminently desirable, bring inequality, which is not. The brief, politically egalitarian world of Macondo's prehistory does not solve personal problems of love and loss. Literature is a plaything or a desperate contrivance to mask loneliness and impotence. Nor is love the answer. José Arcadio and Rebeca's passion does not prevent him from becoming the model indigenous economic exploiter. But perhaps José Arcadio felt only lust, unlike the true love of Aureliano Babilonia for his aunt. But that passionate love is double-edged, as destructive as it is pleasurable. Nor does it solve the problem of death and loss.

As for happiness, like *Rasselas, Waiting for Godot, Henderson the Rain King,* or Max Apple's "Vegetable Love," *One Hundred Years of Solitude* plays a juggling game with the futile search for an enduring happiness. Misery fills life and frustrates hope, but the vital energy we expend in the search distracts us and procures most of the pleasures we find. Because it is a twentieth-century text, predicated on an expectation of happiness, *One Hundred Years of Solitude* is more severe, less forgiving, than *Rasselas* and much closer to Beckett (as Watson's reading implies in its inadvertent resemblance to serious readings of Beckett). García Márquez satirizes the anodynes of daily occupation. The Buendía family habit of making things in order to unmake them and then remake them is not treated with Johnson's compassion, but with Beckett's contempt. In the mockery of those daily routines, there is a hint that something more profound, more meaningful, ought to fill life.

The usual candidates for filling life with meaning—God, literature, love, politics, money—when the fiction picks them up and turns them over, are revealed, in the fiction as in life, to be partial, incomplete, temporary, or nonexistent. That general truth, a little bitter, is nowhere stated but emerges from countless specific examples of struggling lives. At the same time, implicit in the mockery of characters' life-filling makeshifts is the modern refusal to rest content with the inevitable misery of human life.[3] The mockery assumes that we ought to be doing better, while the repetition recognizes that there is nothing we have not tried. As a species we are quite hopeless.

A pattern of initial promise followed by disillusionment repeats itself throughout the novel, in almost every character, in the life of the town, in the "magic realism" of the text. It is visible in Pilar Ternera's endless waiting for the dark man the cards promised her, in Fernanda's wearing the ermine carnival cape she received from the soldiers when they took her away to become a queen, as she had always been promised. Pick up a character, pick up a life, and you will find the promises of youth thwarted by death, disappointment, or age. Aureliano José is shot on his way to Carmelita Montiel. José Arcadio, the firstborn, returns as a tattooed monster his mother does not recognize. The last José Arcadio, raised to be a pope, discovers that his mother's golden chamberpot is only gilt and his mother's Macondo is a trap. Those characters who are not yet either dead or disappointed have disappeared suspended in time. Álvaro is on a train with no return; Alfonso and Germán left on a Saturday to return on Monday and were never heard of again; Gabriel is writing in Paris in the room where Rocamadour has not yet died. Mercedes, well named ("mercies"), is the last to go, but she too vanishes as if she had never existed.

Like hope, magic realism seduces and disappoints. An appetite for wonders and a desire for the impossible draw us into the fiction, where, ultimately, time after time, those wonders turn on us. The sharpest example is the first and almost the last: the fate of the wondrous magnets, magnifying glass, and false teeth with which the novel begins. José Arcadio Buendía delights and amuses us, and makes us marvel, as those devices set him in motion. He traverses centuries of Western intellectual development with only a gypsy as his link to the traditions of scientific thought. Few moments in the novel convey more devastatingly the arid winds of disillusionment than the gypsies' return to Macondo after the deluge. So isolated and defeated are the inhabitants that the gypsies dazzle them once again with magnets, a magnifying glass, and false teeth (318; 418–19). What had seemed a delightful, comic wonder in its first appearance, so energetic and so hopeful, becomes in its reappearance a sign of decay and decrepitude, of defeat and desertion.

Here the character who follows the pattern of hope succeeded by disillusionment is the reader. When the world of Macondo was new, the reader cared nothing about the promises of progress that stirred José Arcadio Buendía. But when the earliest signs come back again, the reader is dismayed by the same absence of progress that tormented José Arcadio Buendía. The reader's thoughtless delight in nostalgia for the primitive has been unmasked. Delighted and seduced by the promise of progress in fairy-tale leaps and bounds, the reader has been seduced and abandoned.

Yet *One Hundred Years of Solitude* is a novel and not a fable.

Between the first appearance of the gypsies and the last, a history has unfolded that might have come out differently. The colonel in his workshop, Amaranta with her burned hand, Meme in her endless, daring contrivances: there is a sense that each could have been luckier and happier if some particular event, accident, blindness, or twist of character had not prevented it. Interrogated about their motives or inner selves, characters respond with a baffling complexity. How can the Amaranta dreaming of a Roman spring with Pietro Crespi on one page reject him on the next, smiling as she tells him she would not marry him if she were dead?

That final ambiguity suggests that for García Márquez human beings are more than victims of forces, repetitions, families, or geography. Shaped and often distorted by circumstances, each character suffers a form imposed upon him or her by others, but each has also an irreducible essence that resists analysis. It is possible to be so enraptured with repetition in *One Hundred Years of Solitude* that the individuality of details or of characters disappears. But it is not necessary. This novel does not force us to linger over the complexities and nuances of character as many other fictions do, but if we choose to pause, those complexities are there. We make (and consume) fictions to inquire into what it means to live, and we also use fictional characters to instruct ourselves in how to live. If the discussion of characters in fiction is "gossip about people who never existed," that gossip serves the same self-regulatory functions as gossip in life. Every analysis of a character's alternatives limns moral choices.[4]

García Márquez does not provide us, in his text, with a single myth around which to organize our lives (or our reading of the text). Instead, the text supplies multiple possibilities, temporary expedients, real and illusory choices. If none of those possibilities produces an enduring happiness, like the Catalan's mirrored nostalgias, each produces a transient one. If the "wildest and most tenacious love [is] an ephemeral truth in the end," it is a wild and tenacious love until the end (370; 477).

12

Intertextuality from the Bible to Borges,

from Gallegos to the Gallo Capón

In 1953 a very young Roland Barthes declared that "a modern master-piece is impossible." Writing was trapped between two debilitating alternatives: repeating outmoded forms and conventions because the writer did not see that the old forms of the bourgeois myth were dead; or, for the writer who did see the new world as it was, repeating an imitative, out-of-date language, "splendid but lifeless."[1] Whether or not that problem has been solved relative to the French novel, we will let others debate. Certainly one circumstance that enabled Latin Americans to launch masterpieces as Barthes launched his polemic was that history and literature remained to be integrated. In France writing might "absorb the whole identity of a literary work," but in Latin America writing still left some room for history, society, politics, and cultural identity. Nor did Latin American writers suffer from any naïveté about the primacy of writing for writing.

While playing with the paradoxes of language in ways that de-cades later would fascinate Derrida, deconstruction's daddy, Jorge Luis Borges had made new literature out of old, very old books, and he had also transformed the Spanish sentence. For young writers who wanted to represent "the world," he had shown new possibilities for language and writing without encroaching on their territory, that is, history, politics, revolution, society. As Barthes saw and said, the crucial invention was a new language, and language comes only out of language. How was a writer to make a language so old, so heavy with others' words, his own? For Barthes, the writer was trapped between anarchic language and dead language. He did not imagine the possibility of an ironic, imperialist language that would rewrite all of Spanish-American and much of Western literature.

Intertextuality is a term coined by the semiotician Julia Kristeva in 1969, a few years after the publication of *One Hundred Years of Solitude,* and its implications are useful for seeing what García Márquez was up to. Intertextuality widens the range of that respectable figure, allusion, to insist upon the participation of any text in a world of texts. *Allusion* signifies a work's specific citations and references, its use of earlier names, texts, phrases, or structures. Intertextuality adds varieties of allusion that are not ordinarily meant when we say "allusion." It includes internal allusions to the text itself within the text; an author's allusions to his own previous work within the work; the participation of the text in cultural codes such as the conventions of genre and narrative; and the allusions to the text made by later texts, the author's own or other people's.

As the reader of *One Hundred Years of Solitude* knows, the novel anticipates every usage. The novel habitually refers to itself in the narrator's anticipations of what is about to happen; it quotes itself; it parallels itself; it even reads (a version of) itself out loud, when Melquíades recites from his encyclicals to Arcadio. Conspicuously and unmistakably, the narrative also incorporates references to much, if not most, of the author's previous work as journalist and maker of fictions. He thus turns those earlier works, once so respectable in themselves, into adumbrations and anticipations of another, later text. The intertextuality of participation in cultural codes, illustrated by the conventions with which the novel opens, comes with the territory—such intertextuality is a condition of writing at all.

Since the text cannot "contain" references made to it by later texts, readers become the site of intertextuality. Readers of Denise Levertov find the Bible quotes her, while Emily Dickinson echoes Seamus Heaney; Pope and Shakespeare spout clichés that everybody knows, and *Tosca* becomes an intricate tissue of self-reflexive references. Or, as we will see below, the Bible is revealed to be patterned after *One Hundred Years of Solitude*. Criticism allows itself to read *One Hundred Years of Solitude* in the light of work that comes after it. Gone is superstitious adherence to the old-fashioned, conventional procedure of reading later works through the earlier one. (This may sound irrational, but consider that one learns a great deal about a writer by seeing how other, later writers have used him. The best readings may always be the empirical kind practiced by one writer on another or by one writer on himself.) Thus, all texts form a sphere, and one can move across that sphere in any direction and for any distance. The reason the term *intertextuality* is useful for *One Hundred Years of Solitude* is not that the novel provides so many examples of it in operation, but that the term suggests a kind of amorphous inclusiveness that characterizes the way *One Hundred Years of Solitude* swallows up other texts and puts them to use. *One Hundred Years of Solitude* borrows phrases here, names there, and structures throughout, and it makes the range and variety of its borrowings part of its point.

The project of José Arcadio Buendía when we first meet him is to catch up to his own present time in the nineteenth century. The project of the reader is to catch up to Col. Aureliano Buendía as he discovers ice and then as the firing squad aims at him. The project of the novel as a whole is to bring the world of one hundred years of solitude into the present of our own twentieth century. In its parts and as a whole, the novel can be read as an elaborate game of catch-up in which the game is lost before it is started. Even if we catch up, somebody has already been there: that is what catching up means. Everything that can be done has already been done somewhere else. At the end of the novel, we finally read a manuscript written a hundred years earlier in fictional time. We catch up to what Melquíades already knew.

At the outset of the novel, that duplication of effort is emblematized by the skeleton in armor. The memento mori that ends the first paragraph tells an untold story of the exploration of a new world in old armor, of war, conflict, lost love, and solitude. Only one skeleton in armor is found, and his solitude is displaced to his galleon, covered with orchids, where the word *solitude* occurs for the first time in the novel. Macondo is a marginal world, and at least one critic has chided José Arcadio Buendía for listening to his wife and failing to move on, as he wanted, to a more propitious, up-to-date, central place, where he would have had access to the findings of science. Had José Arcadio Buendía made the move, that would have been another story. (*Salaam Bombay?*) The story of Macondo and the Buendías is in part the story of a marginal world recapitulating the experiences of the center, and one of the ways the text acts out that repetition is by recapitulating the literature of the center. Just as José Arcadio Buendía catches up to modernity in his own idiosyncratic way, so this text establishes its modernity by catching up to modern writing in the web formed by Western writing.

To reach its end, *One Hundred Years of Solitude* adopts the narrative frame of the Bible and the plot devices of *Oedipus Tyrannos* and parodies both. These two founding narratives of Western culture provide a double foundation for the novel, and the echoes of both are pervasive and unmistakable. A family doomed to incest and a fatal baby who will bring the line to an end have only one possible origin— literature. Melquíades, our Delphic oracle, dooms the Buendías to their fate—*fatum,* what is spoken—because he says it and improves on Delphi by writing it down (as biblical prophets did). (The curse is more literary than mythic. Like biblical prophecy, the text is tainted by legitimate suspicions that a later editor has improved the accuracy of the original prophet's words. For the modern reader the Oedipus complex is a myth; fatality is a myth, invoked to dispel chance, but a curse on the house of Laios is not. Confusing the idea of fatality with the literal curse of the Oedipus myth leads to all those readings that make it sound as though García Márquez believes in ancestral curses. What survives as archetypal from that myth is fatality and repressed desire, not a curse of the gods.)

With the (parodic) curse of incest trailing the family, the novel invokes the Hellenic origins of Western culture, as does the name Arcadio, from Arcady, that peaceful, pastoral, isolated world in the mountains of central Greece. Nor is Greek science neglected in favor of Greek literature: it is the learning of Thales, the pre-Socratic philosopher who cornered the olive market, predicted eclipses, and introduced geometry (640?–546 B.C.), that Melquíades first brings to Macondo. "All things are full of Gods," said Thales; "the magnet has a soul because it makes the iron move."[2] Somewhat unexpectedly, the Buendía history as a whole parallels the history of Greece: sixth-century science precedes fifth-century literature, which overlaps with a 20-year civil war, the Peloponnesian War (431–404 B.C.). The end of the democracy and "golden age" is followed by foreign invasions, Alexander's Macedonians, the Romans, the Ottomans, and, ultimately, the cultural collapse that grieved Byron and other nineteenth-century Hellenophiles. In other words, the history of Macondo is paradigmatic: it follows a pattern that has been played out before in human history, and not only by Greece. The Macedonians, Romans, and Ottomans followed it, too, not to speak of the Maya, Bantu, Inca, and Easter Islanders.

More specific to the novel is the Hellenic impact on structure, the parodic literalization of anagnorisis and peripeteia in the conclusion. Aureliano Babilonia "discovers" who his parents are, what his relation to his beloved was, and what the cosmic meaning of their union was. He also discovers that he is a character in a writing who cannot get out, and in that discovery he finds an entirely unexpected "reversal" of fortune. Looking into a speaking mirror, he discovers that the mirror is real and he is not.

With a youthful patriarch and founding couple in a world so new that things lack names, the novel shifts to another fundamental text, the Bible. In so doing, it at once doubles its structural principles. If the Hellenic principle is dynamic, the Hebrew structure is more static—it tells us where we are and when it is over. Biblical allusion pervades the text, and it is especially marked whenever a disaster looms on the horizon.

In an intricate mélange of stories from the Pentateuch, the first page sets us in a pre-Adamic world where things still lack names. In the prehistory of Macondo, Ursula and José Arcadio Buendía flee from an original crime, a murder (expulsion from the garden), to a land "that no one had promised them," through a mountainous wilderness with a band of followers (the exodus). There, like Cain, they found a city that will later be visited by plagues (insomnia, proliferation of animals, bananas), floods, and an apocalyptic whirlwind that wipes it off the face of the earth. In its earliest moments, before the beginning of this story, the town was happy. José Arcadio Buendía was a youthful patriarch, no one had died, and they had forgotten original sin. When the novel begins, however, the old serpent has bitten José Arcadio Buendía, who lusts for knowledge. Eventually, his wife finds what he has looked for in vain: not only gold but also the road to civilization. Generations later, the story comes to an end in a book that reveals not the future but the past (like Daniel) and seals it up in a book, like Revelation or Daniel.

By invoking the Bible, García Márquez seems to be invoking the origin of all origins, an absolutely primary time; but for anyone familiar with the textual history of the Bible, to invoke the Bible as *the* beginning is to evoke an endless regress of texts, redactions, and fictive authors. Critics have hastened to point out that there is no primary time in *One Hundred Years of Solitude*. The gypsies show that knowledge, science, society, all exist elsewhere, and that Macondo's experience is not primary but a repetition. The skeleton and the galleon not only confirm that there is a world elsewhere, but they also show that people like the *macondanos* once passed where Macondo now is.

At the metatextual level, the very recognition that Macondo is new depends upon a quotation, a reference to a prior text. That sense of newness, of recent creation, of absolute origins, is an illusion. As far as I know, however, no critic has pointed out that in the Bible, too, the beginning is not the beginning. The first words are not the oldest words in the text or the first words of the world, and this primary, original text is in fact a highly complex editing of many vanished texts. Even more to the point, the first five books of the text are traditionally attributed to an author whose life story, including his death, is told inside those five books.

The Bible is a book of duplications, repetitions, repeated patterns, infinite interpretability, and predictions fulfilled and unfulfilled. There are names for these things when they happen in the Bible, such as hermeneutics and typology. García Márquez takes most of his narrative allusions from the first two books of the Pentateuch, Genesis and Exodus. Also known as the Five Books of Moses and traditionally believed to be written by Moses, the Pentateuch takes the story of mankind and Israel from the creation to the death of Moses outside the promised land. During the Middle Ages, close readers such as Rabbi Ben Ezra were troubled by Moses' recording his own death, by changes in the name for God, and other discrepancies in the text. Such concerns led ultimately, at the end of the seventeenth century, to serious textual criticism and, in the nineteenth, to a new theory of authorship of the Pentateuch, the Graff-Wellhausen or "documentary" hypothesis.

While there is much debate about the details, modern textual criticism of the Bible holds that the Pentateuch is a compilation of four to six narrative traditions, and that the Pentateuch began to assume its modern form after the Babylonian exile (597–38 B.C.E.). Moses, the traditional author of the whole, is usually deprived even of the text most closely associated with him, Deuteronomy, the fifth book. An extraordinarily powerful sermon, unlike anything else in the Penta-teuch, Deuteronomy is ostensibly Moses' last, cautionary words to the children of Israel. He predicts (with great accuracy) their future in the promised land, the benefits if they follow the law, the woes if they break it.[3] At the end of the book, he dies and is buried, no one knows where.

In 2 Kings 22–23, during some much needed repairs of the Temple in the reign of Josiah, a book was discovered that served as the basis for wide-ranging religious reforms (ca. 625 B.C.E.). That book, or its core, is now usually identified with Deuteronomy, and how it got there and who wrote it are questions tactfully passed over in silence. So we have books within books, authors writing themselves in their books,

books with both attributed authors and unknown authors: it has all already been done.

As to the origin of all origins, the Bible begins with the words "In the beginning," but it begins with two "beginning" or creation accounts. Worse, the first account is later (by about 500 years, give or take a century) than the account that follows it. The first, familiar account of the seven days of creation creates man male, female, and nameless on the sixth day. That account postdates the exile and is usually placed about 500 B.C.E. The second account is the equally familiar folktale of Adam, Eve, the serpent, and the naming of the animals. The pre-exilic folktale is usually traced to an oral tradition dating about 950 B.C.E. The later splicing of the two accounts has created an early, if unintended, example of "flashback" technique.[4] At the very beginning, then, the beginning of the beginning, there is textual duplication, and there is no original text. With the Bible demurely adopted as a firm foundation for the narrative, the firm line on which the text relies turns out to be even more slippery than the text constructed along it.

The Bible and the Oedipus myth inform large parts of the text, but the text contains many other literary allusions. Many names are named: Nostradamus with his *Centuries* (the title of his predictions), the venerable Bede with his encyclopedic knowledge, Rabelais, the notorious banana peel for critics—a designation Rabelais would have liked. Others' phrases are rephrased: those of Mallarmé, who read all the books; Gonzalo de Berceo, who wanted a glass of good wine; Hemingway, who likened sex to an earthquake. Deliberately wide, the allusive cast nets Western learning and literature from the Hebrews, the Hellenes, and the Romans. (Horace, Seneca, Ovid, the wise Catalan's favorites, and Aureliano: the first brothers divide the wars of the Romans and the sensuality of the Greeks between them, but the Greek Arcady has paternal priority. Aurelian was the name of one Roman emperor, Aurelius of a more famous, philosophical emperor.) Beyond Greece and Rome, the allusive net catches up the Middle Ages, the Renaissance, and the present.

Intertextuality

The systems of recondite literary and scientific allusion situate Macondo in Western culture—a remote outpost, to be sure, but unmistakably Western. The opening pages of the text are full of learned oddities, but the strangest part of those oddities—astrolabes, sextants, alchemical laboratories, and false teeth—is that they are so familiar. If the reader feels this world is primitive and childlike, it is still the reader's own culture whose childhood García Márquez is evoking. There is no pre-Colombian local history, no Tupac Amaru or Macahueles, not even El Dorado. No spirit of Anahuac or the Chibcha rises to grumble at the events passing by. Of the three conquistadores who converged on Bogotá from three different directions, all searching for the "golden man" (*el dorado*), and all arriving within a few weeks of each other in the early sixteenth century, not one is named. Instead, Sir Francis Drake internationalizes the freebooting enterprise.

The translated text is not laced with untranslated words in italics, nor is there a glossary for the Spanish reader. If the reader needs a glossary, it is not for Ifá, Iyalosha, and Iyaré (from Lydia Cabrera's *Cuentos de jicotea* [Tortoise stories]), but for the heretical sect of the Nasciancenes and Monk Herman. (The Spanish text is laced with words and phrases peculiar to the Colombian coast, and their use has annoyed some readers, from Havana to the Pyrenees. Those "coastalisms" are erased by translation or imperfect Spanish, much as Beckett's Irishisms make an American reader stumble but have no effect on a non-native English speaker other than to exasperate him with the inadequacy of his pocket English dictionary. Joset's edition marks special usages.) It would be surprising if the text did not make an implicit, ironic comment on the relevance and value of Western culture in those allusions to Nostradamus and the Venerable Bede, but through them the text lays claim to the whole of the West. Moreover, it does not attempt to revive or to celebrate a lost indigenous culture.

The absence of a lost indigenous culture has been brilliantly treated by Stephen Minta.[5] Minta is the first critic to put together satisfactorily the features of the insomnia plague—loss of language, loss of memory, loss of consciousness—with the peculiar fact that the insomnia plague is associated with two children of an Indian king, Visitación and Cataure, whom the plague has exiled from their kingdom. They do not bring the insomnia plague, as has sometimes been asserted. Rebeca, whose past has been lost, who understands the Indian language, and who is forced to give up her childish habit of eating dirt, brings the insomnia. It arrives when she is assimilated to the family— that is, when she is brought into the children's room, having given up eating dirt (49; 119), her previous life gone forever. The Indians recognize the plague; they are the ones who know what it is and what it means. They have been padding silently about the margins of the narrative with their own language, but when the plague manifests itself in Rebeca, Visitación explains it to the Buendías.

The plague is the destroyer of culture, and Minta linked it to the Indians as the first victims of it, their languages, cultural memories, and political consciousness erased. Far from being a happy release into mythic natural cycles, insomnia is a descent into cultural and personal idiocy. Cataure, like Álvaro and Gabriel later, flees; Visitación, like the last Aureliano, gives up and waits. As Minta pointed out, such obliteration is still more characteristic of the fate of the Indians of Colombia (or Chile or Argentina) than of the Indians of Mexico, Guatemala, or Peru. Paradoxically, the absence of an *indigenista* or "indianist" element at the center of *One Hundred Years of Solitude* and its replacement by familiar Western artifacts suggest how specifically Colombian a writer García Márquez is.

Hispanic Connections

In *One Hundred Years of Solitude,* García Márquez undertook to rewrite or reread in Macondo not only all of Western literature but also an entire Hispanic tradition. *One Hundred Years of Solitude* synthesizes a hundred years of developments in Latin American writing, and it could scarcely have done so without the stimulation of those developments. García Márquez never set himself to imitate any Latin

American writers as he had imitated Faulkner (in *Leaf Storm*). Nor did he ever try to reform his style by scrutinizing another Latin American's practice, as he did with Hemingway. But he shared the ambitions, interests, and dissatisfactions of many of his contemporaries, both older and younger. Among the older writers who might be singled out are Neruda for ambition, Borges for style, Carpentier and Asturias for folklore, and Carpentier again for "the marvelous real" and an ironic vision of history. All four are writers García Márquez had read; Neruda he adored, Borges he rather disliked, Carpentier and Asturias had impressed him, but none of them had changed his life the way Kafka or Faulkner had when he first read them. They mattered to him, and so to us here, less as influences in the conventional sense than as fellow writers who represented new developments, who shared ambitions and interests, and who provoked the desire to equal or to surpass their achievements.

At the base of *One Hundred Years of Solitude* is the regionalist tradition of Gallegos and Rivera transformed by a modernism so ambitiously allusive that it reaches past the formal structures of the eighteenth- and nineteenth-century novel to the episodic, intertextual chronicles of the Renaissance. Fobbing off the *Quixote* as a translation from the Arabic of Cide Hamete Benengeli, Cervantes long ago invented a fictitious author who happens to be an Arab. His too is the circular conceit of the second part, in which a character, having been written up in a book (the first part), meets other characters who already know him because they have read him. The painter painting himself painting himself and others (and sometimes emerging from the frame, as in Murillo) is a device especially popular in Spanish Renaissance painting.

Those mirroring devices had been revived and revitalized by Argentina's Jorge Luis Borges in the 1930s and 1940s, and to him García Márquez owes much (including Borges's translations into Spanish of Virginia Woolf).[6] Borges, García Márquez said soon after the publication of *One Hundred Years of Solitude,* is "one of the authors I read the most and have read the most and like the least. I read Borges for his extraordinary capacity for verbal artifice: he teaches you how to write, he teaches you how to sharpen the instrument you use to say things."[7] As we will see below, García Márquez made a generous return for what Borges had taught him about "verbal artifice."

If Borges's cerebral inventiveness was, as content, antipathetic, García Márquez had long admired Chile's popular Communist poet of love, despair, politics, and artichokes, Pablo Neruda, even before Neruda took up the Adamic task of naming and representing the totality of Latin America and Chile's political and historical experience in his *Canto general* (1950; General song). That ambition to bring together the personal, the political, the lyrical, the economic, the historical animated many young Latin American writers who were dissatisfied with the way the cultural dissonances of their realities had been rendered.[8] Neruda's poetry reached from the heights of Macchu Picchu to "the green grubs of capital" magotting in Latin America's flesh, from the blood running in the streets of Stalingrad to a pot of geraniums on a window sill.

The capacious inclusiveness of Neruda's project had no obvious equivalent in prose, but a number of novelists had set about dissolving the old dichotomy civilization/barbarism and reevaluating the folkloric and mythic traditions of their nations' diverse cultures. Among the more prominent writers to do so were Guatemala's Miguel Angel Asturias, with his revival of Mayan legend and folklore, and Cuba's Alejo Carpentier, with his interest in Afro-Cuban music and folklore. Asturias merged Mayan rain gods and surrealist techniques, while Carpentier adopted a deeply ironic perspective on the realities and history of Latin America. He also insisted that no surrealist could invent marvels comparable to the "marvelous American reality" ("*lo real maravilloso americano*") that the Latin American writer found before him.

There has long been a strong fantastic element in Portuguese and Spanish writing. The line extends from Cervantes to Souza by way of Machado de Assis, Quiroga, Borges, Bioy Casares, Sábato, Cortázar, Rulfo, Fuentes, Arguedas, Asturias, Onetti, Carpentier, Valenzuela, and Donoso. In the *Quixote,* real reality confronts the imagined reality of books (in a book), but in another age Don Quixote's imaginary reality once represented something like a real reality. Asturias's and Carpentier's practice showed that folkloric realities could be represented without condescending to them, debunking them, or segregating them as supernatural. Other Latin American writers have used the fantastic to represent archaic realities, folkloric beliefs, psychological states, metaphysical propositions, and political events. *One Hundred Years of Solitude* uses the fantastic in all those ways.

García Márquez did not benefit from his contemporaries and his tradition without making a return acknowledgement. Scattered through the text are many references to his contemporaries and his immediate predecessors. José Arcadio meets the ghost ship of Victor Hughes still looking for the way to Guadeloupe from Alejo Carpentier's *Explosion in a Cathedral* (1962). Col. Lorenzo Gavilán, a Mexican revolutionary exiled to Macondo and arrested with José Arcadio Segundo during the banana strike, is also an exile from another novel, Carlos Fuentes's *Death of Artemio Cruz* (1962). Sleeping by day and writing by night surrounded by the smell of boiled cauliflower, Gabriel Márquez finds his way in Paris to the room where Rocamadour, the child in Julio Cortázar's *Hopscotch* (1963), was to die. At a more general level, García Márquez may owe the courage to generalize "solitude" as he does to Octavio Paz.

It is true that "solitude" has been one of the most prominent and persistent words in Spanish poetry and prose at least since Góngora's *Solitudes* (ca. 1612–13). It would be difficult to find any poet in Spanish who has not called at least one poem an "ode to solitude." It is also true that the wife of Col. Aureliano Buendía in the notes for a novel of the 1950s was Doña Soledad and that García Márquez has described his childhood as solitary, both in the Aracataca twilights and the Zipaquirá days and nights. But it is too striking a coincidence that Octavio Paz published his eloquent, much reprinted *Labyrinth of Solitude* in 1959, that García Márquez wrote *One Hundred Years of Solitude* in Mexico, and that the final chapter of Paz's book ("The

Dialectic of Solitude") reads like an abstract of García Márquez's unwritten novel. Certainly there is no better account of solitude in *One Hundred Years of Solitude* than the one Paz wrote before the novel was written.[9] Paz did not "discover" solitude for García Márquez as Columbus discovered the new world for Isabella. Instead, he sanctioned the treatment of solitude as a metaphysical construct, a pervasive malaise of modern Colombian (or, in Paz's case, Mexican) experience that subsumed under one term many contradictory, individual experiences. He found solitude for García Márquez as Columbus found the new world for Cortés and Pizarro: he located it; they mapped it, explored it, and peopled it.

Finally, there is Borges. Without Borges's fictions, labyrinths, and infinite Babylonian libraries, his invented worlds with real encyclopedias, hermetic references, and intricate narrative involutions, half of *One Hundred Years of Solitude* would be unimaginable. In García Márquez's work prior to *One Hundred Years of Solitude* there is no hermeticism, no obscure, learned allusion. The filiation in the later work is pure Borges, and García Márquez makes that very clear in the manuscripts of Borges's fellow poet Melquíades.[10] They are written in codes that only Borges could have invented, except, of course, that Borges did not and García Márquez did: "in Sanskrit . . . his mother tongue [with] the even lines in the private cipher of the Emperor Augustus and the odd ones in a Lacedemonian military code" (382; 491). Even, or especially, the hesitations, false starts, and deadly mistakes of interpretation (or decoding) belong to the master.

In addition to his fantastic metaphysics, Borges has an affinity for (or addiction to) direct, clean, lethal violence quite unlike the murkier, clumsier, messier violence in García Márquez's fictions or the displaced violence that García Márquez frequently practices in his writings. There are few rifle butts or beatings in Borges, but there are many murders with waiting knives. No writer is less like García Márquez in his political, social, amorous, and literary desires and ambitions than Borges, and it is precisely the differences that liberated García Márquez to introduce Borgesian play into a world so much more fleshy, political, and historically critical. When García Márquez received the Nobel Prize in 1982, among his first reactions was, "Why didn't they give it to Borges?"

As in the narrator's relation to the text, the narrator's relation to his allusions is variable and almost always parodic, to the point of self-parody. Gabriel Márquez, for example, is last seen in the room where Cortázar's "Rocamadour was to die." Writing by night, sleeping by day, he seems strikingly isolated from those amusing, talkative expatriates carrying on the endless, pointless, self-regarding conversation in the room where Rocamadour dies unnoticed.[11] Whether we are meant to place Gabriel among them or whether we are to see him as a lonely previous tenant is not clear, but in either case his situation is slightly pathetic and faintly comical. González Echevarría has prickled at what he regarded as countless sardonic references to Carpentier, but García Márquez's references are never reverential, not even the great tribute to Borges. What is "Borgesian" in the manuscripts of Melquíades is precisely what makes them unreadable: dead languages and impenetrable codes. However impudent they may be, the references do suppose that the texts, twisted into unforeseen and disrespectful shapes, are alive, and so the unfortunate Lorenzo Gavilán is made to testify to the bravery of his comrade Artemio Cruz.

One of the texts thus twisted and likely to be overlooked by Anglo-American readers is Rómulo Gallegos's *Doña Bárbara* (1929). When Carlos Fuentes first praised García Márquez in *Siempre!* in 1966, he singled out for congratulation García Márquez's liberation of Latin American fiction from "the heavy hand of Doña Bárbara," antiheroine and title character of Gallegos's great novel of the 1920s. One paradox of the repudiation of *Doña Bárbara* by *One Hundred Years of Solitude*, however, is that Doña Bárbara depends as fully as José Arcadio Buendía on one Melquíades: not Melquíades the gypsy, but Melquíades the Wizard (*El Brujeador*). Both Melquíadeses appear at the very beginning of their texts and establish the terms of power within them. Unlikely to be accidental, such a coincidence suggests the utility of rereading *Doña Bárbara* in terms of *One Hundred Years of Solitude*.

The reader who does so will find a novel that has become more sophisticated since Fuentes had to read it in school (a common, beneficial effect of intertextuality).[12] Novelist, president of Venezuela, and now a literary prize (the Rómulo Gallegos), Gallegos and his novel belong to the period that saw the predicament of Latin America as an internal problem of the cultural conflict between the city and the country, civilization and barbarism. That conflict would be resolved, it was hoped, by the triumph of the city, civilization, Europe. Set in the Venezuelan plains, the novel takes as its project "taking the plains out of a man," subduing the savagery endemic to competition and failure in the countryside. It is easy, says one character, quoting another who has lapsed back into the plains, to take a man out of the plains; the difficulty is to take the plains out of a man. When Fuentes praised García Márquez for lifting the burden of Doña Bárbara, he meant the burden of a negative evaluation of the plains, of folklore, of the primitive—precisely the evaluation that forced Gallegos out of an ironic mode into a realistic one.

Early in the novel there is a retrospective on the history of the plains and the family of the hero. Gallegos's tone is coolly ironic as he recounts the Luzardos' seizing land through a more brutal dispossession of the rightful inhabitants than Doña Bárbara practices. His hero's mission is to regain the title to his own lawlessly acquired lands and to put an end to "the arts that caused himself to rise" a generation or two back. In that chapter there are characters closely related to the Buendías, Venezuelan cousins perhaps. A father and son quarrel mortally because one sides with Spain and the other with the United States in a war that concerns Venezuela not at all. When the father throws a lance at his son's head with such force that the lance remains embedded in the wall, the son leaves home. Later the son provokes the father, and the father returns home to announce, "I have just killed Félix. They are bringing him." He shuts himself up to stare at the lance until he dies, eyes wide open, glaring at the lance forever.

The single-minded obsessiveness, the simple pigheadedness, the admirable tenacity, and the destructive stubbornness of these founders are regarded with an ironic sympathy that characterizes García Márquez's fiction throughout. Gallegos drops this tone after one section, because he has a design on his reader that ironic distance will not permit him to implement. It is that design to which Fuentes objected: "folklore, naturalist testimony, and ingenuous denunciation." Pointing to Gallegos on his first page, García Márquez signals more differences than similarities, but he also reminds us of his affection for a writer he recommended, very left-handedly, for the Nobel Prize in 1950.[13]

He also acknowledges a tradition to which he belongs and that he has helped transform. As has occasionally been remarked, García Márquez is the most traditional and regionalist of his contemporaries. His characters are rural, not urban; their physical, geographical surroundings are used to define them and to establish their limits. The conflict between man and nature as man tries to establish civilization over nature's dead body is central to the continuing struggles of the Buendías against ants and laxity. But García Márquez has married Gallegos to the story of the "gallo capón," the story of the castrated cock, or capon. In that endless children's game, the narrator refuses to use language in the ordinary way, for conventional purposes, so that it is invisible. Instead, language is foregrounded, and the story never begins. It is one of those games children love to play when they first realize that language can be used *not* to signify.

Unlike the story of the capon, which is never told, García Márquez satisfies readers (and frustrates critics) by telling many stories. Open-ended, signifying nonsignification, the story of the capon never starts, so it can neither progress nor return to its origin. Language frustrates language's purposes, as gelding frustrates nature's and a cock's. *One Hundred Years of Solitude* slams shut with a finality that closes the book forever, yet multiplies significations even as we look at it. In *One Hundred Years of Solitude,* literature is foregrounded, and the story never quite ends. It is a game adults love to play because it shows, quite effortlessly for the reader, how many ways language can be made to signify and how many things literature can be about.

13

A Second Opportunity on Earth

For I pray God to bless improvements in gardening till London
be a city of palm-trees.
                                                —Christopher Smart[1]

If García Márquez does have a single, modern myth for us, it may be the
desirability of preserving, fostering, nurturing our sense of unreality.
Neither the real world in which we are mired nor the books we read
to remove ourselves, temporarily, to a better world should be entirely
believed.[2] When the wise Catalan loses his "marvelous sense of unreality," he articulates the rational, realistic fatality that *One Hundred
Years of Solitude* inculcates at every level, social, political, personal,
and textual, up to the ending that erases Macondo and the Buendías.
Novels usually show a protagonist overcoming circumstances that seek
to define, control, and limit him or her, even if he or she has to die to
overcome those circumscribing forces. Unbearable to many readers in
the ending of *One Hundred Years of Solitude* is the absence of such
empowerment. Instead of overcoming the world through the fiction,
the Buendías and the last surviving Buendía are overwhelmed by both
the world (a cyclone) and a fiction. A manuscript that should be a means
to liberation becomes eternal confinement, and our last surviving hero
is controlled by a book, rather than liberated through one.

Yet the grim limitations of that reality do not define the experience
of the novel or even its ending. The curious mirroring effect of Mel-

quíades's manuscript brings into play another perspective that reverses, as mirrors will, the dismal fatality of the end of the novel. Following the Möbius strip (Patricia Tobin's fine image), we find ourselves just on the other side. The city will be banished from men's memories, it is foreseen, when Aureliano reaches the last verse; but the city about to be razed has not been erased. Instead, only now is it entering memory as the book ends and Macondo's history passes into the reader's memory. Reading calls Macondo *back* from exile, back from banishment, thrusting its buried men (and women, too) "back in the human mind again." The text makes an assertion that deliberately contradicts the reader's experience of the text. Both cannot be true. The contradiction puts in question fatality—everything "foreseen" in the predication of the sentence—and it restores freedom by limiting doom to an act of imagination.

In his acceptance speech for the Nobel Prize in 1982, García Márquez insisted that it is necessary to believe the impossible in order to stave off the inevitable: "Faced with this awesome reality [mankind's power to destroy his species] that must have seemed a mere utopia through all of human time, we, the inventors of tales, who will believe anything, feel entitled to believe that it is not yet too late to engage in the creation of the opposite utopia. A new and sweeping utopia of life, where no one will be able to decide for others how they die, where love will prove true and happiness be possible, and where the races condemned to one hundred years of solitude will have, at last and forever, a second opportunity on earth."[3]

To pull off that trick will require more imagination, resourcefulness, dexterity, love, and legerdemain than are contained even in *One Hundred Years of Solitude*. If survival really depends on love being true and happiness possible, we are doomed indeed. A world where no one decides for others how they die is "no place" (*utopia*) men have ever been, except Gulliver on his trip to Houyhnhnmland, and no man or race has ever had a second opportunity on earth. Believing these things is to "believe anything." We are equally doomed, however, if we resign ourselves to what, realistically, we know to be inevitable.

The one fantasy García Márquez does not allow his readers is the one that mistakes books for reality. Although Aureliano Babilonia is trapped forever in *One Hundred Years of Solitude,* the reader reading him reading himself knows better and knows more. Among the things his reader should know is that neither reading nor writing novels will save the world (only literary criticism can do that, if we are to believe what we read). Our world will not be saved by acts of the imagination; but neither will it be saved without them. If we hope to avoid the inevitable by accomplishing the impossible, we will continue to need, married to the industry of Ursula, imaginations that go beyond the genius of nature and even beyond miracles and magic.

One Hundred Years of Solitude allows its real readers no place to rest, neither in the imaginary nor in the real. Some readers, it is true, may prefer to remain in the mirrored room with Aureliano Babilonia. The text does not allow it: such readers are thrust out when the city of mirrors becomes a city of sentences. Propounding no transcendent solutions, the novel empowers the imagination, enlarges the resources of literature, and makes us mindful of the existence of multiple realities. These are among the gifts of the active, restless, moving surface that is *One Hundred Years of Solitude.*

NOTES AND REFERENCES

1. From Bloomsbury to Barranquilla

1. Plinio Apuleyo Mendoza, *El olor de la guayaba: Conversaciones con Plinio Apuleyo Mendoza* (Buenos Aires: Editorial Sudamericana, 1982) (*The Fragrance of Guava: Conversations with Plinio Apuleyo Mendoza,* trans. T. Nairn [London: Verso, 1983],) 67–68. Translations are my own unless otherwise noted. Woolf's sentence reads a little differently in English: "But there could be no doubt that greatness was seated within; greatness was passing, hidden, down Bond Street, removed only by a hand's breadth from ordinary people who might now, for the first and last time, be within speaking distance of the majesty of England, of the enduring symbol of the state which will be known to curious antiquaries, sifting the ruins of time, when London is a grass-grown path and all those hurrying along the pavement this Wednesday morning are but bones with a few wedding rings mixed up in their dust and the gold stoppings of innumerable decayed teeth" (*Mrs. Dalloway* [New York: Harcourt, Brace & World, 1925], 23).

2. These names are chosen at random from the copious allusions in García Márquez's early coastal journalism.

3. The invasions of Mexico, Nicaragua, and Guatemala are not forgotten in Latin America as they are in the United States. In 1903 U.S. interference cost Colombia the territory that became Panama. While Colombia has historically suffered less than other countries in Latin America from U.S. economic exploitation, García Márquez's banana zone was the region most affected.

4. For firsthand accounts of what the Cuban revolution meant in its time, see the essays by Padilla (p. 99), Nicolás Guillén (p. 107), Cardenal (p. 207), Skármeta (pp. 252–55), and Claribel Alegría, (p. 299f.) in Doris Meyer, ed., *Lives on the Line* (Berkeley: University of California Press, 1988). For the way the revolution transformed itself for certain Cuban revolutionaries, see Guillermo Cabrera Infante, *Así en la paz como en la guerra* (1961) and *A View*

of Dawn in the Tropics (1974: trans. 1981), and Carlos Franquí, *Family Portrait with Fidel: A Memoir* (1981; trans. 1984).

5. Enrique Fernández, interview with Gabriel García Márquez, *Village Voice*, 3 July 1984, 46.

2. The Importance of the Work

1. "Angel Gabriel," *London Review of Books,* 16 September–6 October 1982, 3.

2. The presence of new publishing houses in Colombia has been traced to the success of *One Hundred Years of Solitude*. Raymond L. Williams, *Una década de la novela colombiana: la experiencia de los setenta* (A decade of the Colombian novel: the seventies) (Bogotá: Plaza y Janés, 1981), 15–17.

3. Gene Bell-Villada has argued for the influence of *One Hundred Years of Solitude* on writers as diverse as Robert Coover, John Nichols, and John Updike (in his atypical *The Coup*). "García Márquez and the Novel," *Latin American Literary Review* 13, no. 25 (1985), 23. The novel's influence perhaps appears in Carlos Fuentes's "total novel" *Terra Nostra,* and certainly in the work of Chile's Isabel Allende and Nicaragua's Sergio Ramírez. In Colombia writers now repudiate imitation, as Gustavo Álvarez Gardeazábal warns in *El titiretero* (The puppeteer): "You are not going to find any Arab diversions or any Chinese boxes of the kind that novelists use to attract the reader. Your feet will always be on the ground; you won't mount on any flying carpet, nor is it going to rain yellow butterflies from the sky." Gardeazábel's joke is that he provided such diversions in earlier novels. See Seymour Menton, *La novela colombiana, planetas y satélites* (The Colombian novel, planets and satellites) (Bogotá: Plaza y Janés, 1978), 359.

4. The closest we are likely to get is García Márquez's current autobiographical project, memoirs to be published, Shandy-style, every time he has 400 pages ready. Marlise Simons, "García Márquez on Love, Plagues and Politics," *New York Times Book Review,* 21 February 1988, 25.

3. Critical Reception

1. In order of appearance, the translations are in French, Italian, Portuguese, Norwegian, English, Catalan, Bulgarian, Croatian, Czech, Russian, Serbian, Yugoslav, Japanese, Lithuanian, Finnish, Hungarian, Rumanian (home of the Romany gypsies), Slovak, Swedish, Turkish, Dutch, Polish, Danish, Estonian, German, and Persian. And, through the good offices of my colleague Steve Goodwin, there now exists a sentence retranslated into its

Notes and References

original Sanskrit. The list of translations is cribbed from Joset's third edition of *Cien años de soledad,* 48–50.

2. So little known was García Márquez in 1963 that the translator of Enrique Anderson Imbert's *Spanish American Literature: A History* (Detroit: Wayne State University Press) thought that the author of *Withered Leaves (La hojarasca)* was a woman. The error had still not been corrected in the second edition (1969).

3. Reprinted in *Gabriel García Márquez,* ed. Peter G. Earle (Madrid: Taurus, 1981), 93.

4. Quoted in Rita Guibert, *Seven Voices,* tr. Frances Partridge (New York: Alfred A. Knopf, 1973), 64.

5. Klaus Müller-Bergh, "Talking to Carpentier," *Review* 76 (1977), 24.

6. Oscar Collazos, Julio Cortázar, and Mario Vargas Llosa, *Literatura en la revolución, y revolución en la literatura* (Literature in the revolution, and the revolution in literature) (Mexico City: Siglo XXI, 1970), 44, 66, 47–48.

7. *"Saludo al margen,"* *Margen* (Paris) 1 (October–November 1966), quoted in *Latin America in Its Literature,* ed. Ivan A. Schulman, trans. Mary G. Berg (New York: Holmes & Meier, 1980), 60.

8. *Historia de un deicidio* (History of a deicide) (Barcelona: Barral, 1971), 479.

9. In Earle, *Gabriel García Márquez,* 95; Carlos Fuentes, *La nueva novela hispanoamericana* (Mexico, D. F.: Joaquín Mortiz, 1969), 62.

10. Review of *One Hundred Years of Solitude, La Quinzaine Littéraire,* 15–31 December 1970, reprinted in *Review 70,* supplement on García Márquez (1971), 171–74.

11. Gene Bell-Villada, "García Márquez and the Novel," *Latin American Literary Review* 13, no. 25 (1985), 15, reprinted in *Critical Essays on Gabriel García Márquez,* ed. George R. McMurray (Boston: G. K. Hall, 1987), 209–18.

12. *The Boom: A Personal History,* trans. Gregory Kolovakos (New York: Columbia University Press, 1977), 56; *Salmagundi* 82–83 (Spring–Summer 1989), 242.

13. Paz in Guibert, *Seven Voices,* 272.

14. "The First Seven Pages of the Boom," *Latin American Literary Review* 15, no. 29 (January–June 1987), 54.

15. In visual terms, this is a preference for Renaissance perspective over the flat surfaces of medieval, Mughal, Oriental, and some modern painting. The flat, mosaiclike surface also explains why so much commentary on the

novel reads like paraphrase: the critic shifts and recombines parts (paraphrasing all the while) instead of penetrating to some other level.

16. Asturias in Guibert, *Seven Voices*, 174; Carlos Blanco Aguinaga, "Sobre la lluvia y la historia en las ficciones de García Márquez," in *Narradores hispanoamericanos de hoy* (Spanish-American writers today), ed. Juan Bautista Avalle-Arce (Chapel Hill: University of North Carolina Press, 1973), 55–71.

17. Carlos Martínez Moreno and Leopoldo Muller, *Psicoanálisis y literatura en* Cien años de soledad, (Psychoanalysis and literature in *One Hundred Years of Solitude*) 2d ed. (Montevideo: Fundación de Cultura Universitaria, 1971), 60.

18. Cristóbal Sarrias, quoted by Randolph D. Pope, "Transparency and Illusion in García Márquez's *Chronicle of a Death Foretold,*" *Latin American Literary Review* 15, no. 29 (1987), 183.

4. An Imaginary Garden with Real Toads

1. Quotations in the text from *One Hundred Years of Solitude* are from Gregory Rabassa's translation (New York: Harper & Row, 1970), which is usually, though not always, followed. The second page reference is to *Cien años de soledad*, 3d ed., annotated and edited by Jacques Joset (Madrid: Cátedra, 1987), because it is such a pleasure to read Joset's notes at the bottom of the pages.

2. Michael H. Hansell, "Wasp Papier-mâché," *Natural History* (August 1989), 55.

3. In her most familiar literary appearance, the ant is also a perfect social democrat, an efficient, egalitarian anarchist: "Go to the ant, thou sluggard; consider her ways, and be wise, / which, having no guide, overseer, or ruler, / Provideth her meat in the summer, and gathereth her food in the harvest" (Prov. 6:6–8).

4. Quoted in Emir Rodríguez Monegal, *El arte de narrar: diálogos* (The art of narrative: dialogues) (Caracas: Monte Avila, 1968), 217.

5. A Myth of Origins for a Mythic Novel

1. García Márquez in Guibert, *Seven Voices*, 326.

2. This form of the name appears in Apuleyo Mendoza, *El olor de la guayaba* 18. Vargas Llosa gives the name as Nicolás Márquez Iguarán. *Historia de un deicidio*, 13.

3. Hispanic surnames combine the patronymics of both parents: the name of the father's father comes first, followed by the name of the mother's

Notes and References

father. Thus, José Arcadio, the son of José Arcadio Buendía and Ursula Iguarán, could be called either José Arcadio Buendía (using only his father's patronymic) or José Arcadio Buendía Iguarán (using his father's and his mother's patronymics). Gabriel García Márquez may be properly called Gabriel García or Gabriel García Márquez, but never Gabriel Márquez. That is either a feminist subversion that favors the mother's patronymic or an oedipal aggression that eliminates the father's.

    4. "*One Hundred Years of Solitude*: The Last Three Pages," reprinted in McMurray, *Critical Essays on Gabriel García Márquez*, 151. The anecdotes that follow are taken principally from Vargas Llosa, *Historia de un deicidio*, 22–25, 27–28.

    5. *Obra periodística* (Journalistic writings), vol. 1, *Textos costeños* (Coastal texts), ed. Jacques Gilard (Barcelona: Bruguera, 1981), 351, 366, 507.

    6. For a discussion of García Márquez's stylistic development, see Vargas Llosa, *Historia de un deicidio*, or Regina Janes, *Gabriel García Márquez: Revolutions in Wonderland* (Columbia: University of Missouri Press, 1981).

6. A Pig's Tail, a Pig's Eye

    1. García Márquez in Guibert, *Seven Voices*, 314.

    2. "Style and Its Image," in *Literary Style: A Symposium*, ed. Seymour Chatman (New York: Oxford University Press, 1971), 10.

    3. "El arto narrativo y la magia" (Magic and the art of storytelling), in *Obras completas* (Complete works), ed. José Edmundo Clemente IV (Buenos Aires: Emecé, 1967), 91.

    4. Apuleyo Mendoza, *El olor de la guayaba*, 82–83.

    5. Suzanne Jill Levine has related that García Márquez told her that the galleon was taken from an image of a sunken transatlantic liner in Hemingway's "After the Storm." *El espejo hablado* (The speaking mirror), 147, n. 6. Such liners are a favorite motif of García Márquez, and the beaching of another in "The Last Voyage of the Ghost Ship" (1968) is an evident metaphor for the "landing" of *One Hundred Years of Solitude*. Elsewhere, García Márquez has remarked that when he found the galleon he knew at last that the novel was going somewhere (*Olor*, 111). When a transatlantic liner turns into a Spanish galleon, an allusion from the present is transferred to the past, just as the four friends at the end of the novel read ancient literature rather than the moderns that interested the "grupo de Barranquilla."

    6. Suzanne Jill Levine, "*La maldición del incesto en* Cien años de soledad" (The curse of incest in *One Hundred Years of Solitude*), *Revista Iberoamericana* 37 (1971), 711, 724.

7. See Jared M. Diamond, "Founding Fathers and Mothers," *Natural History* 97 (June 1988), 10–15. Suzanne Jill Levine mentions a man in Barranquilla who claimed to have the pig's tail, as well as the discovery in subtropical Venezuela of the lost city of Nueva Tarragona, which supposedly had been devoured by an army of ants. The latter was reported in the *New York Times*. Levine, *El espejo hablado*, 21.

8. *"Las formas de hacer el amor en* Cien años de soledad*"* (How they make love in *One Hundred Years of Solitude*), in Francisco E. Porrata, *Explicación de Cien años de soledad* (Sacramento, Calif.: Porrata y Avendaño, 1976) 63–64.

9. In *Essays on Gabriel García Márquez*, ed. Kemy Oyarzún and William W. Megenney (Riverside, Calif.: University of California Latin American Studies Program, 1984), 33–34. There is a hole in this argument: the one place hurricanes do not hit with great, lethal force is the Atlantic coast of Colombia. A recent tally of 31 Atlantic-Caribbean hurricanes between 1900 and 1983 that left from 7 to 6,000 dead with up to $2.5 billion in property damages lists none in Colombia. *New York Times*, 19 September 1989, 12.

10. In "Montiel's Widow," an unnamed character writes that Parisian butchers put "the biggest and prettiest carnation in the pig's ass."

11. It is hard not to see a little oedipal hostility when Aureliano rereads his mother and father's affair (for us the affair of the butterflies) as a mechanic satisfying his lust on a woman giving herself out of rebellion.

7. A Biographical Reading

1. A distinction should be made here between criticism and scholarship: García Márquez scholars have located the data and shown how pervasive such material is, but García Márquez critics have not produced interpretations that make full use of that scholarship.

2. Edwin Williamson, "Magical Realism and the Theme of Incest in *One Hundred Years of Solitude*," in *Gabriel García Márquez: New Readings*, ed. Bernard McGuirk and Richard Cardwell (Cambridge: Cambridge University Press, 1987), 47.

8. A Political Reading

1. Donald L. Shaw, "Concerning the Interpretation of *Cien años de soledad*," *Ibero-Amerikanisches Archiv* 3, no. 4 (1977), 321–22. Shaw situates the problem beautifully.

2. Several years before the U.S.-supported coup that toppled Salvador

Notes and References

Allende Gossens, the democratically elected, socialist president of Chile, García Márquez predicted that the United States would not tolerate parliamentary socialism in Latin America. García Márquez in Guibert, *Seven Voices*, 333.

3. Kenneth R. Andrews, *Drake's Voyages: A Reassessment of Their Place in Elizabethan Maritime Expansion* (New York: Charles Scribner's Sons, 1967), 25–26, 31, 161, 172–74.

4. Carlos Cortés Vargas, *Los sucesos de las bananeras (Historia de los acontecimientos que se desarrollaron en la zona bananera del Dpto. de Magdalena 13 de noviembre de 1928 al 15 de marzo de 1929)* (Banana Happenings: [A history of the events that unfolded in the banana zone of the Department of Magdalena between 13 November 1928 and 15 March 1929]) (Bogotá: La Lua, 1929). One day, having a copy of this book in my office, I offered to show the map to a student who had come by to discuss the novel. I found Macondo's existing "outside" very exciting; my student declined to look at the map. One person's discovery is another's disillusionment; or, to put the moral another way, making the discoveries yourself is more fun. Burn this book.

5. For a more detailed account, see Regina Janes, "Liberals, Conservatives, and Bananas: Colombian Politics in the Fictions of Gabriel García Márquez," *Hispanófila* 82 (1984), 88, 84–86.

6. The novel contains many allusions later than 1959: the dates of *Explosion in a Cathedral, The Death of Artemio Cruz, Hopscotch*, and "Big Mama's Funeral," as well as Victor Medina, a university student of no prominence until 1965, and, perhaps, the death of Torres in February 1966.

7. Walter J. Broderick, *Camilo Torres: A Biography of the Priest-Guerrillero* (Garden City, N.Y.: Doubleday, 1975), 210, 283. Aurelito attacks a garrison with 21 men; Victor Medina's first operation was an attack on Simacota, January 1965, with 27 men and a girl heading off through the mountains.

8. Cited by Mercado Cardona in *Macondo: Una realidad llamada ficción* (Macondo: a reality called fiction), quoted in Janes, "Liberals, Conservatives, and Bananas," 96, 102. This and the story that follows I have told elsewhere, in the article above and in *Gabriel García Márquez: Revolutions in Wonderland*. It embarrasses me to repeat it, but better I should repeat it than my reader not know it.

9. *The Book of Laughter and Forgetting*, trans. Michael Henry Heim (Baltimore: Penguin, 1980), 3.

10. "*La huelga de la compañía bananera como expresión de lo 'Real Maravilloso' americano en* Cien años de soledad" (The strike against the banana company as an instance of the "Marvelous American Real" in *One Hundred Years of Solitude*) *Bulletin Hispanique* 74 (1972), 379–405.

11. A colleague, Terence Diggory, informed me that, in 1989 in Providence, Rhode Island, an attempt by newsboys to organize for better pay was stymied by the newspaper's contention that it, too, had no workers who deliver papers; it employed independent contractors.

9. Principles of Construction

1. Apuleyo Mendoza, *El olor de la guayaba*, 111.

2. *El olor de la guayaba*, 113. Other factors include the simplicity and the fullness of the text's surface. "García Márquez and the Lost Art of Storytelling," in McMurray, *Critical Essays*, 129–40.

3. Gullón (p. 130).

4. Avendaño (p. 130).

5. Gene Bell-Villada has written well on the significance of names and their confusions; see "Names and Narrative Patterns in *One Hundred Years of Solitude*," *Latin American Literary Review* 9, no. 18 (1981), 37–46.

6. Diachronic: across (*dia-*) time (*chronos*): relating to changes in a system over time, historical. Synchronic: same (*syn-*) time (*chronos*): having to do with the relations between parts of a system existing at one period in time. The terms' current use derives from Saussurean linguistics, in which the historical (diachronic) study of languages is distinguished from the (synchronic) study of a language system at a particular time. *Diachronic* is not a necessary word (*historical* would do as well), but it forms a pretty pair with the necessary *synchronic*, which has no substitute.

7. Lucila Mena, *La función de la historia en* Cien años de soledad (Barcelona: Plaza y Janés, 1979), 17.

8. Josefina Ludmer, Cien años de soledad: *Una interpretación* (Buenos Aires: Editorial Tiempo Contemporáneo, 1972). Lydia D. Hazera, "Estudio sinóptico de las personalidades femeninas," in *Explicación de* Cien años de soledad, ed. Francisco E. Porrata and Fausto Avendaño (Sacramento, Calif.: Porrata y Avendaño, 1976), 151–70.

9. Emily Dickinson remarked that when she read Milton the top of her head came off.

10. Once again, José Arcadio Buendía has been beaten to his discovery. The city of ice comes out of Norse mythology and so, for readers and author, out of a book. If we follow Borges's lead in preferring the astonishing *Quixote* written by a nineteenth-century Frenchman, Pierre Menard, to that more predictable *Quixote* written by a Renaissance Spaniard, then José Arcadio Buendía's imagining a city of ice in the tropics is far more inventive, daring, and imaginative than the far more predictable city of ice imagined by a Norseman.

Notes and References

10. Magic Realism: Does He or Doesn't He?

1. Grethe Jurgens, *Der Wachsbogen*, no. 6 (1932), in Seymour Menton, *Magic Realism Rediscovered, 1918–1981* (Philadelphia: Art Alliance Press, 1983), 40.

2. Menton, *Magic Realism Rediscovered*, 9.

3. Angel Flores, "Magical Realism in Spanish American Fiction," *Hispania* 38 (1955), 191. Flores carries the "magical realist" element back to Columbus and the chroniclers, and he dates its modern appearance from Borges's *La historia universal de la infamia* (Universal history of infamy) in 1935, published two years after Borges had translated Kafka's shorter fictions into Spanish.

4. Antonio Fama illustrates that tendency and also provides a good account of the development of the term, its particular appropriateness to Carpentier, Asturias, and García Márquez, and its difference from Todorov's fantastic. *Realismo mágico en la narrativa de Aguilera Malta* (Magic realism in the narrative of Aguilera Malta) (Madrid: Playor, 1977), 13–33. Flores mentions neither Asturias nor Carpentier and congratulates the magical realists for leaving behind "baroque descriptions" and "*cuadros de costumbres*" (genre painting) (191).

5. A very interesting account of West African and Caribbean magic, as it is practiced today and as it was practiced in the colonial period, appears in V. S. Naipaul's "The Crocodiles of Yamassoukro," in his book *Finding the Center* (New York: Vintage Books, 1986), 87–93, 123–26, 149, 160–66.

6. "*Realismo mágico (con cuatro grabados)*" (Magic realism [with four engravings]), *Revista de Occidente* 5, no. 48 (1927), 275. The principal link between Roh and Flores is that de Chirico was definitive for both. Roberto González Echevarría observes that those who adopted "magic realism" following Flores were ignorant of the earlier use by Roh and the parallel term of Carpentier. *Alejo Carpentier: The Pilgrim at Home* (Ithaca, N.Y.: Cornell University Press, 1977), 110.

7. Menton, *Magic Realism Rediscovered*, 9, 13, 52. Menton's formulations are particularly apt for García Márquez, since he began to write about magic realists who painted well after he had written about those who wrote. Contemporaneous with the magic realists and surrealists was the Prague School, with its parallel insistence on "defamiliarization" as the fundamental literary act.

8. "*La realidad de la irrealidad en* Cien años de soledad" (The reality of the un-real in *One Hundred Years of Solitude*), in Porrata and Avendaño, *Explicación de "Cien años de soledad,"* 102. Enrique Anderson Imbert, "'*El realismo mágico' en la ficción hispanoamericana*" (Magic realism in Spanish-American fiction) *Far-Western Forum* 1, no. 2 (May 1974), 175–86.

141

9. García Márquez's folklore is neither Indian nor African, but syncretic. Deriving principally from Western, Hispanic traditions, it includes adopted practices such as the habit among West African and West Indian women of eating dirt.

10. Miguel Fernández-Braso, interviewer, *Gabriel García Márquez* (Barcelona: Editorial Azul, 1969), 86–87. García Márquez, quoted in Porrata and Avendaño, 103.

11. Williamson, "Magic Realism and the Theme of Incest," 45. Williamson is aware of the difficulties of the term, but he is slipping past those problems to get to his own very interesting argument.

12. *Gabriel García Márquez and the Powers of Fiction*, ed. Julio Ortega with Claudia Elliott (Austin: University of Texas Press, 1988), Acknowledgments (n.p.).

13. "García Márquez and the Reality of Latin America," in Oyarzún and Megenney, *Essays on Gabriel García Márquez*, 4. Alegría's inclusion of authors Flores does not mention indicates how the term has spread.

14. "Beyond Magic Realism: Thoughts on the Art of Gabriel García Márquez," *Books Abroad* 47 (1973), 444. Rabassa has also in view the modern, scientific understanding of time and natural properties (photorefractive crystals, for example, in which crystals propagate light, seek out another beam, and act as mirror to that beam), which goes beyond the limited, "common-sense" perception of most novels.

15. "In the Beginning . . . ," in Oyarzún and Megenney, *Essays on Gabriel García Márquez*, 14–26.

16. Carpentier's discussion of "the marvelous real" was expanded in the collection of essays *Tientos y diferencias* (Tentatives and differences) (1964). See the discussion in González Echevarría, *Alejo Carpentier*, 109–10.

17. An interesting article with precisely this problem is Scott Simpkins, "Magical Strategies: The Supplement of Realism," *Twentieth-Century Literature* 34, no. 2 (Summer 1988), 140–54.

18. Richard A. Watson, "A Pig's Tail," *Latin American Literary Review* 15 (1987), 89–92.

19. "The Heart's Eternal Vow" (review of *Love in the Time of Cholera*), *New York Times Book Review*, 10 April 1988, 1.

1 1. And If He Does, What Does It Mean?

1. Williamson, "Magic Realism and the Theme of Incest," 46. Williamson cites several examples of such interpretations, and others may be found in

Shaw, "Concerning the Interpretation." The reading that follows leaves Rodrigo to the side.

2. If any students have been unlucky enough to have had it put in their heads, they should erase from recollection that old, inapplicable, and supremely puzzling definition of irony as "saying the opposite of what one means." That is a good definition of the blunter sarcasm, but it will never help a reader with a truly ironic text. Does Swift mean in *A Modest Proposal* that people should *not* eat children? The ironic speaker says something *other* than what he means, and the relationship of that *other* to what he actually means is highly variable. Nor is what he actually means always clear or certain: one can always see what the ironist disapproves and sometimes, faintly, what he approves, but how deep is the disapproval? Why does he choose this way to render it? How would he have us change it? These questions are very interesting and very slippery: it is not always possible by indirection to find the ironist's directions out. Where the ironist differs from other writers is that he works explicitly and consciously with the gap between saying and meaning. Reading an ironic text is like ice-skating—it is supremely exhilarating when you've caught on, but if you look at your feet and start wondering about what's making you go, a pratfall is in the offing.

3. And sometimes even to recognize it: What else could lie behind the failure to see that people do drugs because they are "a medicine for the mind. Under the pressure of the cares and sorrows of our mortal condition, men have at all times and in all countries called in some physical aid to their moral consolations,—wine, beer, opium, brandy, or tobacco." Edmund Burke, *Thoughts and Details on Scarcity* (1795), in *Works,* vol. 5 (Boston: Little, Brown, 1894), 164.

4. See Robert Boyers, *After the Avant-Garde* (University Park: Pennsylvania State University Press, 1988), 81–90.

12. Intertextuality from the Bible to Borges

1. *Writing Degree Zero* (1953), in *Writing Degree Zero and Elements of Semiology,* tr. Annette Lavers and Colin Smith (London: Jonathan Cape, 1984), 70–71.

2. W. K. C. Guthrie, *A History of Greek Philosophy I: The Earlier Presocratics and the Pythagoreans* (Cambridge: Cambridge University Press, 1962), 65. Appropriately, Thales's teachings are reported by Aristotle and brought to Macondo by a surrogate for the Arab transmission of classical culture, a gypsy.

3. Some of the woes are magnificent. The climax of one series is that

your city will be razed, you will be carried away in ships and offered for sale as a slave, and no man will buy you (Deut. 28:68).

4. A very good account of these matters can be found in James King West, *An Introduction to the Old Testament*, 2d ed. (New York: Macmillan, 1980). The break in the two creation stories comes at Genesis 2:4a, for those who would like to look over the original duplication. As to the status of this interpretation: 40 years ago, Roman Catholicism rejected the Graff-Wellhausen hypothesis (it now tolerates it), but having had a Jesuit education, García Márquez is more likely than many of his readers to have an inkling of these matters. Even if he does not, or did not have it in mind when he chose his devices, the Biblical structure adds another mirage to the city of mirages.

5. *García Márquez: Writer of Colombia* (New York: Harper & Row, 1987), 153.

6. Well treated in Levine, *El espejo hablado*, 46f., 90–91.

7. Vargas Llosa, *Historia de un deicidio*, 188.

8. As a youth, García Márquez was disrespectful of the Colombian classics and dismissed Rivera and Isaacs with youthful disdain: "Rivera with that thing called *La vorágine*" *(The Vortex*, [1924]), "and Jorge Isaac[s], with *La María*" *(Maria*, [1867]), *Textos costeños*, 268.

9. Lydia B. Hall discusses some of the correspondences in *"Labyrinthine Solitude:* The Impact of García Márquez," *Southwest Review* 58, no. 3 (1973), 253–63.

10. This question has been interetingly debated in *Diacritics* by Gullón, Tobin, and González Echevarría. *One Hundred Years of Solitude* has been described as an "Aleph" of literature by George R. McMurray and Emir Rodríguez Monegal. González Echevarría addresses Melquíades and Borges in "The Novel as Myth and Archive." See the bibliography.

11. Julio Cortázar, *Rayuela (Hopscotch)*, chap. 28. Other examples of self-parody include José Arcadio Segundo's being obsessed with the 3,000 dead, and the ineffectuality of writers compared with nonwriters (Pietro Crespi versus José Arcadio; José Arcadio Buendía before and after he takes to Melquíades's manuscripts; the colonel as poet and as warrior). Even Melquíades ceases to astonish, and his powers wane, when he takes up writing.

12. See Roberto González Echevarría, *"Doña Bárbara* Writes the Plain," *The Voice of the Masters* (Austin: University of Texas Press, 1985), 33–63.

13. *Textos costeños*, 246–47. Faulkner was still living—and the greatest novelist around, said García Márquez—but the Nobel Prize committee never gave the award to the best writer. If they had, Faulkner should have had it, but since they never did, Gallegos was good enough and deserved it. Faulkner was awarded the Nobel in 1950.

Notes and References

13. A Second Opportunity on Earth

1. Christopher Smart, *Jubilate Aguo*, fragment B1, sec. 25.

2. The better world of art means, singly or in any combination, more interesting, intense, intelligent, romantic, dangerous, dirty, murderous, challenging, involving, sexy, witty, heroic, meaningful, religious, just, rich, adventurous, successful, unsuccessful, surprising, word-filled, beautiful, what you will, as indicated by what you read.

3. "The Solitude of Latin America," Nobel lecture (1982), tr. Marina Castañeda, in Ortega, *Gabriel García Márquez and the Powers of Fiction*, 87–92, and in Doris Meyer, ed. *Lives on the Line* (Berkeley and Los Angeles: University of California Press, 1988), 230–34.

SELECTED BIBLIOGRAPHY

All works are listed chronologically.

Primary Works

Spanish Editions

La hojarasca. Bogotá: Sipa, 1955.

El coronel no tiene quien le escriba. Medellín: Aguirre, 1958.

La mala hora. Madrid: Talleres de Gráficas Luis Pérez, 1962. Edition repudiated by García Márquez. D. F.: Era, 1966. Regarded by García Márquez as first edition.

Los funerales de la Mama Grande. Xalapa: Universidad Veracruzana, 1962.

Cien años de soledad, 3d ed., ed. Jacques Joset. Madrid: Ediciones Cátedra, 1987. Some errors, some omissions, but indispensable. Buenos Aires: Sudamericana, 1967. First edition.

Isabel viendo llover en Macondo. Buenos Aires: Estuario, 1967.

Relato de un náufrago . . . Barcelona: Tusquets, 1970.

La increíble y triste historia de la cándida Eréndira y su abuela desalmada. Siete cuentos. Barcelona: Barral, 1972.

Ojos de perro azul. Rosario: Equiseditorial, 1972.

El negro que hizo esperar a los ángeles. Rosario: Alfil, 1972.

Cuando era féliz e indocumentado. Caracas: El Ojo del Camello, 1973.

Chile, el golpe y los gringos. Bogotá: Editorial Latina, 1974.

El otoño del patriarca. Barcelona: Plaza y Janés, 1975.

146

Selected Bibliography

Todos los cuentos de Gabriel García Márquez (1947–1972). Barcelona: Plaza y Janés, 1975.

Crónicas y reportajes. Bogotá: Instituto Colombiano de Cultura, 1976.

Operación Carlota. Lima: Mosca Azul, 1977.

Periodismo militante. Bogotá: Son de Máquina, 1978.

Los Sandinistas. Bogotá: Oveja Negra, 1979.

De viaje por los países socialistas: 90 días en la "Cortina de Hierro," 5th ed. Bogotá: La Oveja Negra, 1980.

Así es Caracas. Caracas: Ateneo de Caracas, 1980.

Crónica de una muerte anunciada. Barcelona: Bruguera, 1981.

Textos costeños, ed. Jacques Gilard. *Obra periodística*, vol. 1. Barcelona: Bruguera, 1981.

Entre cachacos, 2 vols., ed. Jacques Gilard. *Obra periodística*, vols. 3 and 4. Bogotá: Oveja Negra, 1982, 1983.

De Europa y América (1955–1960), 2 vols., ed. Jacques Gilard. *Obra periodística*, vols. 5 and 6. Bogotá: Oveja Negra, 1983, 1984. All volumes indispensable for antecedents and development.

El rastro de tu sangre en la nieve; El verano feliz de la Señora Forbes (screenplay). Bogotá: William Dampier, 1982.

El secuestro: relato cinematográfico. Salamanca: Loguez, 1983. Original title: *Viva Sandino*. Also published as *El asalto: el operativo con que el FSLN se lanzó al mundo*, 2d ed. Managua: Nueva Nicaragua, 1983.

Persecución y muerte de minorías: dos perspectivas polémicas, 4th ed., with Guillermo Nolasco-Juarez. Buenos Aires: Juarez, 1984.

El amor en los tiempos de cólera. Mexico, D.F.: Diana, 1985.

La aventura de Miguel Littín clandestino en Chile. Mexico, D.F.: Diana, 1986.

El general en su laberinto. Buenos Aires: Sudamericana, 1989.

English Translations

No One Writes to the Colonel (El coronel no tiene quien le escriba) and Other Stories, trans. J. S. Bernstein. New York: Harper & Row, 1968. Contains *No One Writes to the Colonel* and the stories of *Big Mama's Funeral*.

One Hundred Years of Solitude (Cien años de soledad), trans. Gregory Rabassa. New York: Harper & Row, 1970.

Leaf Storm (La hojarasca) and Other Stories, trans. Gregory Rabassa. New York: Harper & Row, 1972. Contains *Leaf Storm* and six stories, four written after *One Hundred Years of Solitude* ("The Handsomest Drowned Man in the World," "A Very Old Man with Enormous Wings,"

"Blacamán the Good, Vendor of Miracles" and "The Last Voyage of the Ghost Ship") and two before ("Monologue of Isabel Watching It Rain in Macondo" and "Nabo").

The Autumn of the Patriarch (El otoño del patriarca), trans. Gregory Rabassa. New York: Harper & Row, 1976.

Innocent Eréndira (La increíble y triste historia de la cándida Eréndira y su abuela desalmada) and Other Stories, trans. Gregory Rabassa. New York: Harper & Row, 1978. Contains *Innocent Eréndira*, nine early stories from *Eyes of a Blue Dog*, "The Sea of Lost Time," and "Death Constant beyond Love."

In Evil Hour (La mala hora), trans. Gregory Rabassa. New York: Harper & Row, 1979.

Chronicle of a Death Foretold (Crónica de una muerte anunciada), trans. Gregory Rabassa. New York: Harper & Row, 1982.

Collected Stories (Todos los cuentos de Gabriel García Márquez [1947–1972]), trans. Gregory Rabassa. New York: Harper & Row, 1984.

The Story of a Shipwrecked Sailor (Relato de un náufrago), trans. Randolph Hogan. New York: Alfred A. Knopf, 1986.

Clandestine in Chile: The Adventures of Miguel Littín (La aventura de Miguel Littín clandestino en Chile), trans. Asa Zatz. New York: H. Holt & Co., 1987.

Love in the Time of Cholera (El amor en los tiempos de cólera), trans. Edith Grossman. New York: Alfred A. Knopf, 1988.

The General in His Labyrinth (El general en su laberinto), trans. Edith Grossman. New York: Alfred A. Knopf, 1990.

Secondary Works

Interviews

Harss, Luis, and Barbara Dohman. "The Lost Chord." In *Into the Mainstream*. New York: Harper & Row, 1967.

Mario Vargas Llosa and Gabriel García Márquez. *La novela en America Latina (diálogo)* (The novel in Latin America [a dialogue]). Lima: Carlos Milla Batres, 1968.

Samper, Daniel. "El novelista García Márquez no volverá a escribir" (The novelist García Márquez will not write again). *El Tiempo, lecturas dominicales* (Bogotá), 22 December 1969.

Selected Bibliography

Fernández-Braso, Miguel. *La soledad de Gabriel García Márquez (Una conversacion infinita)* (The solitude of Gabriel García Márquez [an infinite conversation]). Barcelona: Editorial Planeta, 1972, a book-length interview.

Guibert, Rita. *Seven Voices*, trans. Frances Partridge, New York: Alfred A. Knopf, 1973. García Márquez is one of the seven "voices" interviewed.

Kennedy, William. "The Yellow Trolley Car in Barcelona and Other Visions: A Profile of Gabriel García Márquez." *Atlantic Monthly* (January 1973), 50–59.

Rodman, Selden. "Gabriel García Márquez." In *Tongues of Fallen Angels: Conversations.* New York: New Directions, 1974.

García Márquez habla de García Márquez (García Márquez talks about García Márquez). Bogota: Rentería, 1979.

Mendoza, Plinio Apuleyo. *El olor de la guayaba: Conversaciones con Plinio Apuleyo Mendoza.* Buenos Aires: Sudamericana, 1982. *The Fragrance of Guava: Conversations with Plinio Apuleyo Mendoza*, trans. T. Nairn. London: Verso, 1983.

Fernández, Enrique. "The Seductive Life of García Márquez." *Village Voice,* 3 July 1984, 44–47.

Plimpton, George. *Writers at Work*, no. 6. London: Secker and Warburg, 1985.

"Confident Optimism" (Abbreviated Text of Conversation between Mikhail Gorbachev and Colombian Writer Gabriel García Márquez). *Soviet Life* (December 1987), 1.

Simons, Marlise. "García Márquez on Love, Plagues, and Politics." *New York Times Book Review,* 21 February 1988, 1, 23–25.

Williams, Raymond L. "The Visual Arts, the Poetization of Space and Writing: An Interview with Gabriel García Márquez." *Proceedings of the Modern Language Association (PMLA)* 104 (1989), 131–40.

Books

Arnau, Carmen. *El mundo mítico de Gabriel García Márquez* (The mythic world of Gabriel García Márquez). Barcelona: Ediciones Península, 1971.

Bell-Villada, Gene. *García Márquez: The Man and His Work.* Chapel Hill: University of North Carolina Press, 1990. Most complete account to date of García Márquez's life and works. Includes chapters on Colombian politics, culture, and literature and García Márquez's legacy in North American writing.

Benedetti, Mario, et al. *Nueve asedios a García Márquez* (Nine approaches to García Márquez). Santiago: Editorial Universitaria, 1971. Distinguished collection.

Bhalla, Alok. *García Márquez and Latin America.* London: Oriental University Press, 1987.

Brotherston, Gordon. *The Emergence of the Latin American Novel.* Cambridge: Cambridge University Press, 1977.

Carrillo, Germán. *La narrativa de Gabriel García Márquez* (The narrative of Gabriel García Márquez). Madrid: Ediciones de Arte y Bibliofilia, 1975.

Collazos, Oscar. *García Márquez: La Soledad y la Gloria* (García Márquez: the solitude and the glory). Barcelona: Plaza y Janés, 1983. Life and works.

Earle, Peter G., ed. *Gabriel García Márquez.* Madrid: Taurus, 1981. Includes essays by Angel Rama, Volkening, Fuentes, Todorov, Gullón, Rodríguez Monegal, Arenas, Kennedy.

Foster, David William, compiler. *Handbook of Latin American Literature.* New York: Garland, 1987. A valuable guide to Latin American literary history: authors, works, and distinctive national and regional traditions.

Fuenmayor, Alfonso. *Crónicas sobre el Grupo de Barranquilla.* (Stories of the Group of Barranquilla). Bogota: Instituto Colombiano de Cultura, 1978. Formative period in Barranquilla.

Fuentes, Carlos. *La nueva novela hispanoamericana* (The new Spanish-American novel). Mexico, D.F.: Editorial Joaquín Mortiz, 1969. "The second reading."

———. *Gabriel García Márquez and the Invention of America.* Liverpool: Liverpool University Press, 1987.

Gallagher, D. P. *Modern Latin American Literature.* New York: Oxford University Press, 1973. Fine chapter on *Cien años de soledad* (reprinted in McMurray, *Critical Essays*).

Giacoman, Helmy F., ed. *Homenaje a Gabriel García Márquez* (Homage to Gabriel García Márquez). New York: Las Américas, 1972.

Gullón, Ricardo. *García Márquez o el olvidado arte de contar* (García Márquez; or, the lost art of storytelling). Madrid: Taurus, 1970. Narrative techniques.

Halka, Chester S. *Melquíades, Alchemy, and Narrative Theory: The Quest for Gold in* Cien años de soledad. Lathrup Village, Mich.: International Book Publishers, 1981.

Janes, Regina. *Gabriel García Márquez: Revolutions in Wonderland.* Columbia: University of Missouri Press, 1981.

Selected Bibliography

Karsen, Sonja. *Ensayos de literatura e historia iberoamericana (Essays on Iberoamerican Literature and History)*. New York: Peter Lang, 1988.

Levine, Suzanne Jill. *El espejo hablado* (The speaking mirror). Caracas: Monte Avila, 1972.

Ludmer, Josefina. Cien años de soledad: *Una interpretación (One Hundred Years of Solitude*: an interpretation). Buenos Aires: Tiempo Contemporáneo, 1972. Excellent structuralist reading.

McGuirk, Bernard, and Richard Cardwell, eds. *Gabriel García Márquez: New Readings*. Cambridge: Cambridge University Press, 1987. Valuable collection. Includes García Márquez's Nobel address.

McMurray, George R. *Critical Essays on Gabriel García Márquez*. Boston: G. K. Hall, 1987. Includes essays by Coover, Kazin, Rodríguez Monegal, Bell-Villada, Grossman, Gullón, Gallagher, and Ciplijauskaité.

———. *Gabriel García Márquez*. New York: Ungar, 1977.

McNerney, Kathleen. *Understanding Gabriel García Márquez*. Columbia: University of South Carolina Press, 1989.

Mena, Lucila. *La función de la historia en* Cien años de soledad (The function of history in *One Hundred Years of Solitude*). Barcelona: Plaza y Janés, 1979.

Minta, Stephen. *García Márquez: Writer of Colombia*. New York: Harper & Row, 1987. Valuable on Colombian contexts.

Mose, Kenrick, E. A. *Defamiliarization in the Works of Gabriel García Márquez: 1947–1967*. Lewiston, N.Y.: Edwin Mellen Press, 1989.

Oberhelman, Harley D. *The Presence of Faulkner in the Writings of García Márquez*. Lubbock: Texas Tech Press, 1980.

Ortega, Julio. *Poetics of Change: The New Spanish-American Narrative*, tr. Galen D. Greaser. Austin: University of Texas Press, 1984.

———, with Claudia Elliott, eds. *Gabriel García Márquez and the Powers of Fiction*. Austin: University of Texas Press, 1988.

Oyarzún, Kemy, and William W. Megenney, eds. *Essays on Gabriel García Márquez*. Riverside: University of California Latin American Studies Program, 1984. Morello-Frosch on critical reading, and Alegría and Menton on magic realism.

Palencia-Roth, Michael. *Gabriel García Márquez: la línea, el círculo, y las metamorfosis del mito* (Gabriel García Márquez: the line, the circle, and the metamorphoses of myth). Madrid: Gredos, 1983.

———. *Myth and the Modern Novel: García Márquez, Mann, and Joyce*. New York: Garland, 1987.

Porrata, Francisco E., ed. *Explicación de* Cien años de soledad *de García*

Márquez (Explication of *One Hundred Years of Solitude*). Sacramento, Calif.: Porrata y Avendaño, 1976. Valuable collection.

Scheweitzer, S. Alan. *Three Levels of Reality in García Márquez's* Cien años de soledad. Madrid: Plaza Mayor Ediciones, 1972.

Segre, Cesare. *Semiotics and Literary Criticism*. The Hague: Mouton, 1973. "Curved Time."

Shaw, Bradley, and Nora Vera-Godwin, eds. *Critical Perspectives on Gabriel García Márquez*. Lincoln: University of Nebraska Press, 1986.

Shaw, Donald L. *Nueva narrativa hispanoamericana* (New Spanish-American narrative). Madrid: Cátedra, 1981.

Tobin, Patricia Drechsel. *Time and the Novel: The Genealogical Imperative*. Princeton, N.J.: Princeton University Press, 1978.

Vargas Llosa, Mario. *García Márquez: Historia de un deicidio*. Barcelona: Barral, 1971. Fundamental account of the life and works. Some factual errors.

Williams, Raymond L. *Gabriel García Márquez*. Boston: Twayne, 1984. Dialogism and periodical journalism.

Bibliographies

Fau, Margaret Eustella. *Gabriel García Márquez: An Annotated Bibliography, 1947–1979*. Westport, Conn.: Greenwood Press, 1980.

———, and Nelly Sfeir de González. *Bibliographic Guide to Gabriel García Márquez, 1979–1985*. Westport, Conn.: Greenwood Press, 1986.

Articles

Barros-Lémez, Alvaro. "Beyond the Prismatic Mirror: *One Hundred Years of Solitude* and Serial Fiction." *Studies in Latin American Popular Culture* 3 (1984), 105–14.

Bell-Villada, Gene. "García Márquez and the Novel." *Latin American Literary Review*, 13, no. 25 (January–June 1985), 15–23. Fine account of reception and influence (reprinted in McMurray, *Critical Essays*).

Brushwood, John. "Two Views of the Boom: North and South." *Latin American Literary Review* 15, no. 29 (January–June 1987), 13–31.

Dilmore, Gene. "*One Hundred Years of Solitude*: Some Translation Corrections." *Journal of Modern Literature* 11, no. 2 (July 1984), 311–14. Useful, though incomplete.

Selected Bibliography

Dixon, Paul B. "Joke Formulas in *Cien años de soledad.*" *Chasqui* 15, nos. 2–3 (February—May 1987), 15–22.

Foppa, Aleída. "La crítica francesa de *Cien años de soledad*" (French criticism of *One Hundred Years of Solitude*). In *III Congreso Latinoamericano de Escritores* (Caracas: Ediciones del Congreso de la República, 1971), 187–91.

Gass, William. "The First Seven Pages of the Boom." *Latin American Literary Review* 15, no. 29 (January–June 1987), 33–56. Seven openings of seven novels.

Gilard, Jacques. "El Grupo de Barranquilla." *Revista Iberoamericana* 50, nos. 128–29 (July–December 1984), 905–35.

González Echevarría, Roberto. "Polemic: With Borges in Macondo." *Diacritics* 2, no. 1 (Spring 1972), 57–60.

———. "*Cien años de soledad*: The Novel as Myth and Archive." *Modern Language Notes* 99, no. 2 (1984), 358–80.

Gullón, Ricardo. "Gabriel García Márquez and the Lost Art of Storytelling." *Diacritics* 1, no. 1 (1971), 27–32.

Janes, Regina. "Liberals, Conservatives, and Bananas: Colombian Politics in the Fictions of Gabriel García Márquez." *Hispanófila* 82 (1984), 79–102.

McMurray, George R. " 'The Aleph' and *One Hundred Years of Solitude*: Two Microscopic Worlds." *Latin American Literary Review* 13, no. 25 (1985), 55–64.

Merrel, Floyd. "José Arcadio Buendía's Scientific Paradigms: Man in Search of Himself." *Latin American Literary Review* 2, no. 4 (1974), 59–70. Arab transmission of ideas to the West.

Rodríguez Monegal, Emir. "Novedad y anacronismo de *Cien años de soledad.*" *Nueva narrativa hispanoamericana* 1, no. 1 (1971), 17–39. In Giacoman, *Homenaje.* Translated by author as "A Writer's Feat," *Review 70*, no. 3 (1971), 122–28.

———. "*One Hundred Years of Solitude*: The Last Three Pages." *Books Abroad* (1973), 485–89. Best account of the novel's ending (reprinted in McMurray, *Critical Essays*).

Santos Calderón, E. "Alternativa: 6 años de compromiso" (Alternative: 6 years of commitment). *Alternativa*, no. 257 (27 March 1980). Retrospective, in final issue.

Shaw, Donald. "Concerning the Interpretation of *Cien años de soledad.*" *Ibero-Amerikanisches Archiv* 3, no. 4 (1977), 317–29. Excellent account of three levels of interpretation: epistemelogical, ontological, and historical.

Simpkins, Scott. "Magical Strategies: The Supplement of Realism." *Twentieth-Century Literature* 34, no. 2 (1988), 140–54.

Tobin, Patricia. "García Márquez and the Genealogical Imperative." *Diacritics* 4, no. 2 (1974), 52–55.

Todorov, Tzvetan. "Macondo en Paris." In *Gabriel García Márquez,* ed. Peter G. Earle. Madrid: Taurus, 1981.

Watson, Richard A. "A Pig's Tail." *Latin American Literary Review* 15, no. 29 (1987), 89–92. Brilliant, parodic analysis.

INDEX

Index

157

Index

THE AUTHOR

Regina Janes is professor of English at Skidmore College. She received her B.A. from the University of California at Berkeley (1967) and her M.A. and Ph.D. degrees from Harvard University (1968, 1972). A member of Phi Beta Kappa, she held a fellowship from the National Endowment for the Humanities in 1981–82.

She is the author of *Gabriel García Márquez: Revolutions in Wonderland* and numerous articles, including interviews with Guillermo Cabrera Infante and Carlos Fuentes. Her research interests include eighteenth-century English literature and modern Spanish-American literature. Her articles and reviews have appeared in journals such as *Hispania, Hispanófila, Chasqui, World Literature Today, Salmagundi, Representations, Novel, Journal of the History of Ideas, Eighteenth-Century Studies, The Scriblerian,* and *Notes and Queries.*